CONTENTS ✔ KT-116-865

PREFACE

This revised and enlarged edition is the latest in a long line of Hugo phrase books and is of excellent pedigree, having been compiled by experts to meet the general needs of tourists and business travellers. Arranged under the usual headings of 'Hotels', 'Motoring' and so forth, the ample selection of useful words and phrases is supported by a 2,000 line mini-dictionary. By cross-reference to this, scores of additional phrases may be formed. There is also an extensive menu guide listing approximately 600 dishes or methods of cooking and presentation.

Highlighted sections illustrate some of the replies you may be given and the signs or instructions you may see or hear. The pronunciation of words and phrases in the main text is imitated in English sound syllables, and particular characteristics of French are illustrated in the Introduction. You should have no difficulty managing the language, especially if you use our audio-cassette of selected extracts from the book. Ask your bookseller for the Hugo French Travel Pack.

Hugo's Simplified System

French
Phrase Book

Hugo's Language Books Limited

This revised edition
© 1993 Hugo's Language Books Ltd/Lexus Ltd
All rights reserved
ISBN: 0 85285 196 7

4th impression 1996

Compiled by
Lexus Ltd
with
Valérie Dupin
and
Karen McAulay

*Facts and figures given in this book were
correct when printed. If you discover any
changes, please write to us.*

Set in 9/9 Plantin and Plantin Light by
Lexus Ltd with Dittoprint Ltd, Glasgow
Printed in Great Britain

INTRODUCTION

PRONUNCIATION

When reading the imitated pronunciation, the same value should be given to all syllables as there is practically no stress in French words. Pronounce each syllable as if it formed part of an English word, and you will be understood sufficiently well. Remember the points below, and your pronunciation will be even closer to the correct French. Use our audio-cassette of selected extracts from this book, and you should be word-perfect!

AN represents the nasal sound as in **vin**, **un**, **combien**, **plein** and **main** – similar to saying 'an' without sounding the 'n'

g is pronounced hard as in 'get'

I pronounced as 'eye'

ʒ like the 's' sound in 'leisure'

ON represents the nasal sound as in **bon**, **combien**, **en**, **temps**, **franc**, and **ambulance** – similar to saying 'on' without sounding the 'n'

OO is how we imitate the French 'u' (say 'seen' with your lips rounded as if you were about to whistle, and the result will be close enough)

USE OF THE FRENCH WORD 'ON'

Phrases involving 'I' or 'we' and impersonal phrases have sometimes been translated with the French word 'on', for example: **Can I camp here?** Est-ce qu'on peut camper ici ?. Literally, 'on' means 'one' but is not a formal word as it is in English.

GENDERS AND ARTICLES

French has two genders for nouns – masculine and feminine. In this book, we generally give the definite article ('the') – **le** for masculine nouns, **la** for feminine nouns and **les** for plural nouns. Where the indefinite article ('a', 'an') is more appropriate, we have given **un** for masculine and **une** for feminine nouns or the words for 'some', **du** (masculine), **de la** (feminine) and **des** (plural).

USEFUL EVERYDAY PHRASES

YES, NO, OK ETC

Yes/no
Oui/non
wee/nON

Excellent!
Parfait !
parfeh

Don't!
Non !
nON

OK
D'accord
dakkor

That's fine
C'est bien
seh byAN

That's right
C'est exact
set exakt

GREETINGS, INTRODUCTIONS

How do you do, pleased to meet you
Enchanté (de faire votre connaissance)
ONshONtay duh fair vottr konnessONss

Good morning
Bonjour
bONjoor

Good evening/Good night
Bonsoir
bONswahr

Goodbye
Au revoir
oh-rvwahr

How are you?
Comment allez-vous ?
kommONt allay voo

(familiar form)
Comment vas-tu ?
kommON va tOO

My name is ...
Je m'appelle ...
juh mappell

What's your name?
Comment vous appelez-vous ?
kommON vooz appellay voo

(familiar form)
Comment tu t'appelles ?
kommON tOO tappell

What's his/her name?
Comment s'appelle-t-il/s'appelle-t-elle ?
kommON sappellteel/sappelltell

May I introduce ...?
Puis-je vous présenter ... ?
pweeJ voo prayzONtay

This is ...
Voici ...
vwah-see

Hello/Hi!
Bonjour/Salut !
bONJoor/salOO

Bye!/Cheerio!
Salut !
salOO

7

See you later
A bientôt
ah byANtoh

It's been nice meeting you *(said by a man/woman)*
J'ai été heureux/heureuse de faire votre connaissance
Jay aytay uhruh/uhruhz duh fair vottr konnessONss

PLEASE, THANK YOU, APOLOGIES

Thank you/No thank you
Merci/Non merci
mairsee/nON mairsee

Please
S'il vous plaît
seel voo pleh

Excuse me!/Sorry!
Pardon !
pardON

I'm really sorry
Je suis vraiment désolé
Juh swee vraymON dayzolay

It was my fault/it wasn't my fault
C'était de ma faute/ce n'était pas de ma faute
sayteh duh ma foht/suh nayteh pa duh ma foht

WHERE, HOW, ASKING

Excuse me please
Pardon
pardON

Can you tell me ...?
Pouvez-vous me dire ... ?
poovay voo muh deer

Do you mind if I smoke?
Cela ne vous ennuie pas que je fume ?
suhla nuh vooz ONwee pa kuh juh fOOm

I don't eat meat or fish
Je ne mange ni viande ni poisson
juh nuh mONj nee vee-ONd nee pwass-ON

What would you like to drink?
Qu'est-ce que vous voulez boire ?
kesskuh voo voolay bwahr

I would like a …
Je voudrais un/une …
juh voodreh AN/OOn

Nothing for me thanks
Rien pour moi, merci
ryAN poor mwah mairsee

I'll get this one
C'est moi qui offre
seh mwah kee offr

Cheers! *(toast)*
Santé !
sONtay

I would like to …
J'aimerais …
jemmereh

Let's go to Versailles/the cinema
Allons à Versailles/au cinéma
allONz ah vairsI/oh seenayma

Let's go swimming/for a walk
Allons nager/nous balader
allON najay/noo baladay

11

What's the weather like?
Quel temps fait-il ?
kell tON feteel

The weather's awful
Le temps est affreux
luh tON et affruh

It's pouring down
Il pleut à verse
eel pluh a vairs

It's really hot/it's very sunny
Il fait vraiment chaud/il fait beaucoup de soleil
eel feh vrehmON shoh/eel feh bohkoo duh solay

HELP, PROBLEMS (see also EMERGENCIES p108)

Can you help me?
Pouvez-vous m'aider ?
poovay voo mayday

I don't understand
Je ne comprends pas
juh nuh kONprON pa

Do you speak English/German/Spanish?
Est-ce que vous parlez anglais/allemand/espagnol ?
esskuh voo parlay ONgleh/allmON/espan-yol

Does anyone here speak English?
Est-ce qu'il y a quelqu'un ici qui parle anglais ?
esskeel-ya kellkAN ee-see kee parl ONgleh

I can't speak French
Je ne parle pas français
juh nuh parl pa frONseh

I don't know
Je ne sais pas
juh nuh seh pa

What's wrong?
Qu'est-ce qui ne va pas ?
kesskee nuh va pa

Please speak more slowly
Pouvez-vous parler plus lentement, s'il vous plaît ?
poovay voo parlay plOO lONtmON seel voo pleh

Please write it down for me
Pouvez-vous me l'écrire, s'il vous plaît ?
poovay voo muh laykreer seel voo pleh

I've lost my way
Je me suis perdu
juh me swee pairdOO

Go away!
Allez-vous-en !
allay vooz ON

TALKING TO RECEPTIONISTS ETC

I have an appointment with ...
J'ai rendez-vous avec ...
jay rONdayvoo avek

I'd like to see ...
J'aimerais voir ...
jemmereh vwahr

Here's my card
Voici ma carte
vwah-see ma kart

My company is ...
Ma compagnie est ...
ma kONpan-yee eh

May I use your phone?
Est-ce que je peux utiliser votre téléphone ?
esskuh Juh puh OOteeleezay vottr taylayfon

THINGS YOU'LL HEAR

à bientôt	see you later
attention !	look out!
au revoir	goodbye
bien	fine
bon !	right!, OK!
bonjour	hello
bon voyage !	have a good trip!
c'est correct	that's right
comment allez-vous ?	how are you?
comment ça va ?	how are things?
de rien	you're welcome
enchanté	pleased to meet you
entrez	come in
excusez-moi	excuse me
je ne comprends pas	I don't understand
je ne sais pas	I don't know
je suis vraiment désolé !	I'm so sorry!
je vous en prie	don't mention it
merci	thank you
merci beaucoup	thank you very much
merci, pareillement	thank you, the same to you
non	no
oui	yes
papiers, s'il vous plaît	your identity papers, please
pardon !/pardon ?	sorry!/pardon?
précisément	exactly

→

prenez	help yourself
qu'est-ce que vous avez dit ?	what did you say?
ravi de faire votre connaissance	how do you do, nice to meet you
salut !	hi!; cheerio!
si	yes
très bien, merci – et vous ?	very well, thank you – and you?
voici	here you are
vraiment ?	is that so?

THINGS YOU'LL SEE

accueil	reception
ascenseur	lift
à vendre	for sale
caisse	till, cash desk
complet	full, no vacancies
dames	ladies
défense de …	… forbidden
eau non potable	not drinking water
eau potable	drinking water
emplacement réservé	no parking
en dérangement/en panne	out of order
entrée	entrance, way in
entrée gratuite	admission free
entrée libre	admission free
entrez sans frapper	enter without knocking
fermé	closed
fermeture annuelle	annual closure
fermeture automatique des portes	doors close automatically
frappez avant d'entrer	knock before entering
fumeurs	smoking

→

15

heures de visite	visiting hours
heures d'ouverture	opening times
il est interdit de marcher sur les pelouses	keep off the grass
interdiction de fumer	no smoking
interdit(e)	forbidden, prohibited
jour férié	public holiday
libre	free, vacant
messieurs	gents
ne pas … sous peine d'amende	… will be fined
non-fumeurs	no smoking
occupé	engaged
ouvert	open
passage interdit	no entry
payez ici	pay here
peinture fraîche	wet paint
poussez	push
premier étage	first floor
prière de …	please …
privé	private
renseignements	enquiries
réservé	reserved
rez-de-chaussée	ground floor
route	road
rue	street
rue piétonne/rue piétonnière	pedestrian precinct
sans issue	dead end
sortie	exit
sortie de secours	emergency exit
sous-sol	basement
syndicat d'initiative	tourist information
tirez	pull
veuillez …	please …

COLLOQUIALISMS

You may hear these: to use some of them yourself could be risky!

arnaque	rip-off, swindle
bagnole	car
balles	francs
barbant	deadly boring
bécane	bike
bon sang de merde !	bloody hell!
borne	kilometre
bouffe	food
bourré	pissed
ça alors !	I don't believe it!
c'est pas mon truc	it's not my sort of thing
chiche !	you're on!
cinglé	nutter, nutcase
copain	pal, mate
crado	filthy
crevé	knackered
débloquer: tu débloques !	you're crazy!
dingue	crazy
fringues	gear, togs
génial !	great!, fantastic!
machin	thing, thingummy
mec	bloke
merde !	shit!
mioche	kid, brat
nana	bird
paumé	done for, had it
pote	pal, mate
prendre un pot	to have a drink
salaud	bastard
super !	great!
sympa	nice
truc	thing, thingummy
vachement ...	bloody ..., damn(ed) ...

17

DAYS, MONTHS, SEASONS

Sunday	dimanche	*deemONsh*
Monday	lundi	*lANdee*
Tuesday	mardi	*mardee*
Wednesday	mercredi	*mairkruhdee*
Thursday	jeudi	*Juhdee*
Friday	vendredi	*vONdruhdee*
Saturday	samedi	*sammdee*
January	janvier	*JONvee-ay*
February	février	*fayvree-ay*
March	mars	*marss*
April	avril	*ahvreel*
May	mai	*meh*
June	juin	*JwAN*
July	juillet	*Jwee-ay*
August	août	*oo*
September	septembre	*septONbr*
October	octobre	*oktobr*
November	novembre	*novONbr*
December	décembre	*dayssONbr*
Spring	le printemps	*prANtON*
Summer	l'été	*laytay*
Autumn	l'automne	*lohton*
Winter	l'hiver	*leevair*
Christmas	Noël	*noh-el*
Christmas Eve	le réveillon de Noël	*rayvay-yON duh noh-el*
Good Friday	Vendredi saint	*vONdredee sAN*
Easter	Pâques	*pak*
New Year	le nouvel an	*noovel ON*
New Year's Eve	le réveillon de nouvel an	*rayvay-yON duh noovel ON*
Whitsun	la Pentecôte	*pONtkoht*

18

NUMBERS

0 zéro *zayro*
1 un, une *AN, OOn*
2 deux *duh*
3 trois *trwah*
4 quatre *kattr*
5 cinq *sANk*
6 six *seess*
7 sept *set*
8 huit *weet*
9 neuf *nuhf*

10 dix *deess*
11 onze *ONz*
12 douze *dooz*
13 treize *trez*
14 quatorze *kattorz*
15 quinze *kANz*
16 seize *sez*
17 dix-sept *deess-set*
18 dix-huit *deess-weet*
19 dix-neuf *deess-nuhf*

20 vingt *vAN*
21 vingt et un *vANtay AN*
22 vingt-deux *vAN duh*
30 trente *trONt*
40 quarante *karrONt*
50 cinquante *sANkONt*
60 soixante *swassONt*
70 soixante-dix *swassONt-deess*
80 quatre-vingts *kattruhvAN*
90 quatre-vingt-dix *kattruh-vANdeess*
100 cent *sON*
110 cent-dix *sONdeess*
200 deux cents *duh-sON*
1,000 mille *meel*
10,000 dix mille *deess meel*
20,000 vingt mille *vAN meel*
100,000 cent mille *sON meel*
1,000,000 un million *meel-iON*

19

TIME

today	aujourd'hui	*ohʒoord-wee*
yesterday	hier	*yair*
tomorrow	demain	*duhmAN*
the day before yesterday	avant-hier	*avONt-yair*
the day after tomorrow	après-demain	*apreh-duhmAN*
this week	cette semaine	*set suhmen*
last week	la semaine dernière	*suhmen dairnee-air*
next week	la semaine prochaine	*suhmen proshen*
this morning	ce matin	*suh mattAN*
this afternoon	cet après-midi	*set apreh-meedee*
this evening/ tonight	ce soir	*suh swahr*
yesterday afternoon	hier après-midi	*yair apreh-meedee*
last night	hier soir	*yair swahr*
tomorrow morning	demain matin	*duhmAN mattAN*
tomorrow night	demain soir	*duhmAN swahr*
in three days	dans trois jours	*dON trwah ʒoor*
three days ago	il y a trois jours	*eelya trwah ʒoor*
late	tard	*tar*
early	tôt	*toh*
soon	bientôt	*byANtoh*
later on	plus tard	*plOO tar*
at the moment	pour le moment, maintenant	*poor luh momON, mANtnON*
second	une seconde	*suhgONd*
minute	une minute	*meenOOt*
ten minutes	dix minutes	*dee meenOOt*
quarter of an hour	un quart d'heure	*kar dur*
half an hour	une demi-heure	*duhmee ur*

20

three quarters of an hour	trois quarts d'heure	*trwah kar dur*
hour	une heure	*ur*
day	un jour	*Joor*
every day	chaque jour	*shak Joor*
all day	toute la journée	*toot la Joornay*
the next day	le lendemain	*luh lONduhmAN*
week	une semaine	*suhmen*
fortnight	quinze jours,	*kANz Joor,*
	deux semaines	*duh suhmen*
month	un mois	*mwah*
year	une année, un an	*annay, ON*

TELLING THE TIME

The 24-hour clock is always used in the written form in timetables and for appointments, and also verbally in enquiry offices and if talking about the times of television and radio programmes. However, in most other situations people will use the 12-hour clock.

'What time is it?' is **quelle heure est-il?**. 'O'clock' is translated by **heure(s)**, meaning 'hour(s)'. '(It's) one o'clock' is **(il est) une heure**; '(it's) four o'clock' is **(il est) quatre heures** and so on.

To say 'half past', use **et demie**, so 'half past five' is **cinq heures et demie**.

To express minutes past the hour, state the hour followed by the number of minutes; for example 'ten past five' is **cinq heures dix**. For minutes to the hour use **moins**, which means 'less'; for example 'twenty to eleven' is **onze heures moins vingt**.

'Quarter' is **quart**, so 'quarter past three' is **trois heures et quart**, and 'quarter to eight' is **huit heures moins le quart**.

The word 'at' in phrases such as 'at quarter past two' can be translated by **à**: **à deux heures et quart**.

The expressions 'am' and 'pm' have no exact equivalents but the words **du matin** 'in the morning', **de l'après-midi** 'in the afternoon', **du soir** 'in the evening' or 'at night' are used to distinguish between times that might otherwise be confused. For

21

example, '5 am' is **cinq heures du matin** and '5 pm' is **cinq heures de l'après-midi**; '11 am' is **onze heures du matin** and '11 pm' is **onze heures du soir**.

am	du matin	*dOO matAN*
pm *(afternoon)*	de l'après-midi	*duh lapreh-meedee*
(evening)	du soir	*dOO swahr*
one o'clock	une heure	*OOn ur*
ten past one	une heure dix	*OOn ur deess*
quarter past one	une heure et quart	*OOn ur ay kar*
twenty past two	deux heures vingt	*duhz ur vAN*
half past one	une heure et demie	*OOn ur ay duhmee*
twenty to two	deux heures moins vingt	*duhz ur mwAN vAN*
quarter to two	deux heures moins le quart	*duhz ur mwAN luh kar*
two o'clock	deux heures	*duhz ur*
13.00 (1 pm)	treize heures	*trez ur*
16.30 (4.30 pm)	seize heures trente	*sez ur trONt*
at seven o'clock	à sept heures	*ah set ur*
noon	midi	*meedee*
midnight	minuit	*meenwee*

THE CALENDAR

The cardinal numbers on page 19 are used to express the date in French with the exception of 'the first' when the ordinal number is used:

the first of June	le premier juin	*luh pruhm-yay JwAN*
the second of August	le deux août	*luh duh oo*
the twentieth of May	le vingt mai	*luh vAN meh*
the twenty first of May	le vingt-et-un mai	*luh vANt ay AN meh*

HOTELS

France has over 17,000 hotels officially classified as Tourist Hotels by the Ministère du Commerce. These are identified by a blue and white hexagonal-shaped sign which shows the exact category of the hotel. These categories are: one star HRT: plain but fairly comfortable hotel; two stars HT: good, average hotel; three stars HGTGC: very comfortable; four stars HTGC: top class hotel; L: luxury hotel.

In addition to the officially classified Tourist Hotels there are many others in which the rates, services and amenities differ considerably. Among these are:

Relais de Tourisme: hotel with a limited number of rooms but offering food of a very good standard.

Relais Routiers: hotels, but mainly restaurants, situated on main roads. The food is excellent, the accommodation very reasonable, and the prices surprisingly low.

Relais Châteaux: usually of a very high standard and situated in beautiful and historical surroundings, they provide first-rate food.

Relais de Campagne: these are close to the main highways; most of them are in picturesque settings and all provide excellent food.

Logis et Auberges de France: this independent chain of mostly 1- and 2-star hotels situated off the beaten track gives the motorist a rare opportunity to explore the deep countryside. They have to comply with a rigid set of standards as regards food, service and sanitation in order to get financial assistance from the State. The rates are very reasonable.

USEFUL WORDS AND PHRASES

balcony	un balcon	*balkON*
bathroom	la salle de bain	*sal duh bAN*
bed	le lit	*lee*
bed and breakfast	gîte et petit déjeuner	*Jeet ay puhtee day-Juhnay*

23

bedroom	la chambre	*shONbr*
bill	la note	*not*
breakfast	le petit déjeuner	*puhtee day-ʒuhnay*
car park	le parking	*par-keeng*
dining room	la salle à manger	*sal ah mONʒay*
dinner	le dîner	*deenay*
double bed	un lit de deux personnes	*lee duh duh pairson*
double room	une chambre pour deux personnes	*shONbr poor duh pairson*
foyer	le hall de réception	*ohl duh raysseps-iON*
full board	la pension complète	*pONss-iON kONplet*
guesthouse	une pension de famille	*pONss-iON duh famee*
half board	la demi-pension	*duhmee pONss-iON*
hotel	un hôtel	*oh-tell*
key	la clé, la clef	*klay*
lift	l'ascenseur	*assONssur*
lounge	le salon	*salON*
lunch	le déjeuner	*day-ʒuhnay*
maid	la femme de chambre	*fam duh shONbr*
manager	le directeur	*deerektur*
receipt	le reçu	*ruh-sOO*
reception	la réception	*raysseps-iON*
receptionist	le/la réceptionniste,	*raysseps-ioneest*
room	la chambre	*shONbr*
room service	le service en chambre	*sairveess ON shONbr*
shower	la douche	*doosh*
single bed	un lit d'une personne	*lee dOOn pairson*
single room	une chambre pour une personne	*shONbr poor OOn pairson*
toilet	les toilettes	*twallet*
twin room	une chambre à deux lits	*shONbr ah duh lee*

Have you any vacancies?
Avez-vous des chambres de libres ?
avay voo day shONbr duh leebr

I have a reservation
J'ai réservé
Jay rayzairvay

I'd like a single room
Je voudrais une chambre pour une personne
Juh voodreh OOn shONbr poor OOn pairson

I'd like a room with a bathroom/balcony
Je voudrais une chambre avec salle de bain/balcon
Juh voodreh OOn shONbr avek sal duh bAN/balkON

I'd like a room for one night/three nights
Je voudrais une chambre pour une nuit/trois nuits
Juh voodreh OOn shONbr poor OOn nwee/trwah nwee

What is the charge per night?
Quel est le prix pour une nuit ?
kell eh luh pree poor OOn nwee

I don't know yet how long I'll stay
Je ne sais pas encore combien de temps je vais rester
Juh nuh seh paz ONkor kONbyAN duh tON Juh veh restay

When is breakfast/dinner?
A quelle heure servez-vous le petit déjeuner/le dîner ?
ah kell ur sairvay voo luh puhtee day-Juhnay/luh deenay

Please wake/call me at seven o'clock
Réveillez-moi à sept heures, s'il vous plaît
rayvay-yay mwah ah set ur seel voo pleh

Can I have breakfast in my room?
Pouvez-vous servir mon petit déjeuner dans la chambre ?
poovay voo sairveer mON puhtee day-Juhnay dON la shONbr

I'll be back at ten o'clock
Je serai de retour à dix heures
Juh suhray duh ruhtoor ah deess ur

25

My room number is 205
Le numéro de ma chambre est le deux cent cinq
luh nOOmayroh duh ma shONbr eh luh duh sON sANk

I'd like to have some laundry done
J'aimerais faire laver du linge
Jemmereh fair lah-vay dOO lANJ

My booking was for a double room
J'ai réservé une chambre pour deux personnes
Jay rayzairvay OOn shONbr poor duh pairson

I asked for a room with an en-suite bathroom
J'ai demandé une chambre avec salle de bain attenante
Jay duhmONday OOn shONbr avek sal duh bAN attuhnONt

I need a light bulb
Il me faut une ampoule
eel muh foh OOn ONpool

There is no toilet paper in the bathroom
Il n'y a pas de papier toilette dans la salle de bain
eel nya pa duh papee-ay twalet dON la sal duh bAN

The window won't open
Pas moyen d'ouvrir la fenêtre
pa mwI-AN doovreer la fuhn-ettr

There isn't any hot water
Il n'y a pas d'eau chaude
eel nya pa doh shohd

The socket in the bathroom doesn't work
La prise dans la salle de bain ne marche pas
la preez dON la sal duh bAN nuh marsh pa

I'm leaving tomorrow
Je pars demain
Juh par duhmAN

26

When do I have to vacate the room?
A quelle heure dois-je libérer la chambre ?
ah kell ur dwah juh leebayray la shONbr

Can I have the bill please?
Pouvez-vous préparer ma note, s'il vous plaît ?
poovay voo prayparay ma not seel voo pleh

I'll pay by credit card
Je payerai avec une carte de crédit
juh pay-uhray avek OOn kart duh kraydee

I'll pay cash
Je payerai comptant
juh pay-uhray kONtON

Can you get me a taxi?
Pouvez-vous m'appeler un taxi ?
poovay voo mapplay AN taxee

Can you recommend another hotel?
Pouvez-vous recommander un autre hôtel ?
poovay voo ruhkommONday AN oht-r oh-tell

THINGS YOU'LL SEE

addition	bill
ascenseur	lift
chambre à deux lits	twin room
chambre pour deux personnes	double room
chambre pour une personne	single room
complet	no vacancies
déjeuner	lunch
demi-pension	half board
douche	shower
entrée	entrance

→

27

entrée interdite	no admission
escalier	stairs
gîte et petit déjeuner	bed and breakfast
maison d'hôtes	guesthouse
pension	guesthouse
pension complète	full board
pension de famille	guesthouse
petit déjeuner	breakfast
poussez	push
privé	private
réservé	reserved
réservé au personnel	staff only
réservé aux clients de l'hôtel	hotel patrons only
salle de bain	bathroom
sortie de secours	emergency exit
tirez	pull

REPLIES YOU MAY BE GIVEN

Je suis désolé, mais nous sommes complets
I'm sorry, we're full

Nous n'avons plus de chambres pour deux personnes/une personne
There are no double/single rooms left

Pour combien de nuits ?
For how many nights?

Comment payez-vous ?
How will you be paying?

Veuillez payer d'avance
Please pay in advance

La chambre doit être libérée à midi
You must vacate the room by midday

CAMPING AND CARAVANNING

Campsites: there are more than 6,000 recognised campsites in France, graded from 1 to 4 stars. Most of these have an enclosure under constant supervision, running water, washing places, wash houses, hygienic lavatories, a refuse clearance service and facilities for buying food in or near the camp.

Youth hostels: there are more than 300 youth hostels in France which are available to anybody who holds a YHA membership card. This card can be obtained in the UK and is valid all over the world. Most French hostels provide only the bare essentials. For further information you should consult your own Youth Hostel Association or the Fédération Unie des Auberges de la Jeunesse.

USEFUL WORDS AND PHRASES

bucket	un seau	soh
campfire	un feu de camp	fuh duh kON
go camping	faire du camping	fair dOO kONpeeng
campsite	un terrain de camping	terrAN duh kONpeeng
caravan	une caravane	karavan
caravan site	un terrain de camping/caravaning	terrAN duh kONpeeng/ karavaneeng
cooking utensils	des ustensiles de cuisine	OOstONseel duh kweezeen
drinking water	de l'eau potable	oh pot-abl
ground sheet	un tapis de sol	tapee duh sol
hitch-hike	faire de l'autostop	fair duh loh-tohstop
rope	une corde	kord
rubbish	les ordures	ordOOr
rucksack	un sac à dos	sak ah doh
saucepans	des casseroles	kassrol
sleeping bag	un sac de couchage	sak duh kooshaJ
tent	une tente	tONt
youth hostel	une auberge de jeunesse	oh-bairJ duh Juhness

Can I camp here?
Est-ce qu'on peut camper ici ?
esskON puh kONpay ee-see

Can we park the caravan here?
Est-ce qu'on peut garer la caravane ici ?
esskON puh garray la karavan ee-see

Where is the nearest campsite/caravan site?
Où se trouve le terrain de camping/caravaning le plus proche ?
oo suh troov luh terrAN duh kONpeeng/karavaneeng luh plOO prosh

What is the charge per night?
Quel est le prix pour une nuit ?
kell eh luh pree poor OOn nwee

How much is it for a week?
Ça coûte combien pour une semaine ?
sa koot kONbyAN poor OOn suhmen

I only want to stay for one night
Je veux rester une nuit seulement
Juh vuh restay OOn nwee suhlmON

We're leaving tomorrow
Nous partons demain
noo partON duhmAN

Where is the kitchen?
Où est la cuisine ?
oo eh la kweezeen

Can I light a fire here?
Est-ce que je peux allumer un feu ici ?
esskuh Juh puh allOOmay AN fuh ee-see

Do you know where I can get ...?
Est-ce que vous savez où je peux trouver ... ?
esskuh voo savay oo Juh puh troovay

Is there drinking water here?
Est-ce qu'il y a de l'eau potable ici ?
esskeel-ya duh loh pot-abl ee-see

THINGS YOU'LL SEE

allumer	to light
à louer	for hire
auberge de jeunesse	youth hostel
camping interdit	no camping
couverture	blanket
cuisine	kitchen
douches	showers
eau non potable	not drinking water
eau potable	drinking water
emplacement	site
entrée	entrance
feu	fire
gérant	manager
lavoir	washing place
lumière	light
recharge	refill
réchaud à gaz	calor gas stove
remorque	trailer
sac de couchage	sleeping bag
sanitaires	toilets and showers
tente	tent
terrain de camping	campsite
toile de tente	tent

VILLAS AND APARTMENTS

Self-catering accommodation is widely available and can be a villa, a small cottage, a flat or part of a farmhouse.

You may be asked to pay for certain 'extras' not included in the original price. You might want to ask if electricity, gas etc is included. It's a good idea to ask about an inventory at the start, rather than be told something is missing later just as you are about to leave. You may be asked for a deposit – so make sure you get a receipt for this.

USEFUL WORDS AND PHRASES

agent	un agent	aʒON
bath *(tub)*	la baignoire	ben-ywahr
bathroom	la salle de bain	sal duh bAN
bedroom	la chambre à coucher	shONbr ah kooshay
blind	le store	stor
blocked	bouché	booshay
boiler	le chauffe-eau	shohff oh
break	casser	kassay
broken	cassé	kassay
caretaker	le/la concierge	kONsee-airʒ
central heating	le chauffage central	shohffaʒ sONtrahl
cleaner	la femme de ménage	fam duh maynaʒ
cooker	la cuisinière	kweezeenee-air
deposit	la caution	kohss-iON
drain	l'égout	aygoo
dustbin	la poubelle	poobel
duvet	la couette	koo-et
electrician	l'électricien	aylektreess-yAN
electricity	l'électricité	aylektreess-eetay
fridge	le frigo	freegoh
fusebox	la boîte à fusibles	bwat ah fOOzeeb-l
gas	le gaz	gaz
grill	le gril	greel

32

heater	le radiateur	*radee-atur*
iron	le fer à repasser	*fair ah ruhpassay*
ironing board	la planche à repasser	*plONsh ah ruhpassay*
keys	les clés	*klay*
kitchen	la cuisine	*kweezeen*
leak *(noun)*	la fuite	*fweet*
(verb)	couler	*koolay*
light	la lumière	*lOOmee-air*
light bulb	l'ampoule	*ONpool*
living room	la pièce de séjour	*pee-ess duh sayJoor*
maid	la femme de chambre	*fam duh shONbr*
pillow	l'oreiller	*oray-yay*
pillow slip	la taie d'oreiller	*teh doray-yay*
plumber	le plombier	*plONb-yay*
refund	le remboursement	*rONboorsmON*
sheets	les draps	*drah*
shower	la douche	*doosh*
sink	le lavabo	*lavaboh*
stopcock	le robinet d'arrêt	*robeenay dar-reh*
swimming pool	la piscine	*peeseen*
swimming pool engineer	le technicien responsable de la piscine	*tekneess-yAN ruhsponsab-l duh la peeseen*
tap	le robinet	*robeenay*
toilet	les toilettes	*twalet*
towel	la serviette	*sairvee-et*
washing machine	la machine à laver	*masheen ah lavay*
water	l'eau	*oh*
water heater	le chauffe-eau	*shohff oh*

Does the price include gas/electricity/cleaning?
Est-ce que le prix comprend le gaz/l'électricité/le nettoyage ?
esskuh luh pree kONprONd luh gaz/laylektreess-eetay/luh nettwah-yaJ

33

Do I need to sign an inventory?
Est-ce que je dois signer un état des lieux ?
esskuh Juh dwah seen-yay AN ayta day lyuh

Where is this item?
Où se trouve cet objet ?
oo suh troov set obJay

Please take it off the inventory
Pouvez-vous le retirer de l'état des lieux ?
poovay voo luh ruhteeray duh layta day lyuh

We've broken this
Nous avons cassé ceci
nooz avON kassay suhsee

This was broken when we arrived
C'était cassé quand nous sommes arrivés
sayteh kassay kON noo somz arreevay

This was missing when we arrived
Ça n'y était pas quand nous sommes arrivés
sa nyay-teh pa kON noo somz arreevay

Can I have my deposit back?
Puis-je récupérer ma caution ?
pweeJ raykOOpayray ma kohss-iON

Can we have an extra bed?
Pourrions-nous avoir un lit supplémentaire ?
pooree-ON nooz avwahr AN lee sOOplaymONtair

Can we have more crockery/cutlery?
Pourrions-nous avoir plus de vaisselle/couverts ?
pooree-ON nooz avwahr plOO duh vess-el/koovair

Where is …?
Où se trouve … ?
oo suh troov

When does the maid come?
Quand vient la femme de chambre ?
kON vee-AN la fam duh shONbr

Where can I buy/find ...?
Où est-ce que je peux acheter/trouver ... ?
oo esskuh Juh puh ashuhtay/troovay

How does the water heater work?
Comment est-ce que le chauffe-eau fonctionne ?
kommON esskuh luh shohff oh fONkss-iON

Do you do baby-sitting?
Est-ce que vous gardez les enfants ?
esskuh voo garday layz ONfON

Do you prepare lunch/dinner?
Est-ce que vous préparez le déjeuner/le dîner ?
esskuh voo prayparay luh day-Juhnay/luh deenay

Do we have to pay extra or is it included?
Est-ce que nous devons payer un supplément, ou est-ce que
c'est compris ?
esskuh noo duhvON pay-ay AN sOOplaymON oo eskuh seh kompree

The shower doesn't work
La douche ne marche pas
la doosh nuh marsh pa

The sink is blocked
Le lavabo est bouché
luh lavaboh eh booshay

The sink/toilet is leaking
L'évier/le W.-C. coule
layvyay/luh vay say kool

There's a burst pipe
Une canalisation a sauté
OOn kanaleezass-iON ah sohtay

35

The rubbish has not been collected for a week
Depuis une semaine les ordures n'ont pas été enlevées
duhpwee OOn suhmen layz ordOOr nON paz aytay ONluhvay

There's no electricity/gas/water
Il n'y a pas d'électricité/de gaz/d'eau
eel nya pa daylektreess-eetay/duh gaz/doh

The bottled gas has run out – how do we get a new cylinder?
Il n'y a plus de gaz – comment pouvons-nous procurer une nouvelle bouteille ?
eel nya plOO duh gaz – kommON poovON noo prokOOray OOn noovel bootay

Can you mend it today?
Pouvez-vous le réparer aujourd'hui ?
poovay voo luh rayparay ohJoordwee

What is the name and telephone number of the nearest doctor/dentist?
Pouvez-vous me donner le nom et numéro de téléphone du docteur/dentiste le plus proche ?
poovay voo muh donnay luh nON ay nOOmayroh duh taylayfon dOO doktur/dONteest luh plOO prosh

Send your bill to …
Envoyez votre facture à …
ONvwah-yay vottr faktOOr ah

I'm staying at …
Je loge au …
Juh loJ oh

Thanks for looking after us so well
Merci de vous être si bien occupé de nous
mairsee de vooz ettr see byAN okOOpay duh noo

See you again next year
A l'année prochaine
ah lannay proshen

Drive on the right, overtake on the left. A solid line in the centre of the road must never be crossed. Overtaking when there is a solid central line is a serious offence and can result in an on-the-spot fine. A broken central line may be crossed for the purpose of overtaking another vehicle or for crossing the road. Double lines, one solid and the other broken, may be crossed only where the broken line is immediately to the driver's left. Double lines must not be crossed when the solid line is nearest to the driver's left-hand side.

The use of the horn is very frequent in France (especially in Paris) even if the **code de la route** (highway code) forbids it. Seat belts must be worn at all times.

Speed limits: In built-up areas vehicles must not exceed 50 km/h (31 mph). Some urban areas have a lower speed limit than this, which is indicated at the point where it comes into force. Outside urban areas the speed limits are as follows: toll motorways 130 km/h (81 mph); free motorways and dual carriageways 110 km/h (68 mph); all other roads outside towns 90 km/h (56 mph). These limits apply also to motor bikes over 81cc; lighter machines (51cc-80cc) are restricted to 75 km/h (46 mph) while mopeds up to 50cc may not travel faster than 45 km/h (28 mph). On wet roads, speed limits are reduced from 130 to 110 km/h, from 110 to 100 km/h and from 90 to 80 km/h.

Right of way: In built-up areas you must give way to vehicles coming out of a turning on your right. On some roundabouts you may have priority, or you may see a sign saying **vous n'avez pas la priorité** (below the usual roundabout symbol in a red triangle) – meaning you must give way. Outside built-up areas, your priority is indicated by **passage protégé** below a crossroads sign, or by the familiar broad arrow crossroads sign, or by a yellow diamond sign.

Motorways: There are two types of motorway in France: the **autoroutes de dégagement** which are found around towns and which are free, and the **autoroutes de liaison** or **autoroutes à**

péage which are toll motorways. The French motorway network is well spread over the country and allows quick access to most French **régions**. The most important are: **l'autoroute du Nord** (Paris-Lille), **l'autoroute de l'Est** (Paris-Strasbourg), **l'autoroute du Soleil** (Paris-Marseilles), **la Languedocienne** (Orange-Le Perthus), **l'Aquitaine** (Paris-Bordeaux) and **l'Océane** (Paris-Nantes).

Parking: Drivers must park on the right-hand side of the road in the direction the car is travelling.

In towns, parking is usually restricted between 9 am and 12.30 pm and 2.30 pm and 7 pm during week days. You may have to use a **parcmètre** (parking meter) or pay for parking - **parking payant** - this can mean taking a ticket on arrival and paying on departure. In areas covered by **horodateurs**, you will have to buy a ticket and display it.

Documentation: you must carry with you the original vehicle registration document, a full valid national driving licence and current insurance certificate.

Fines: you can be fined on the spot for exceeding the drink driving limit (the limit is the same as in the UK), speeding and not wearing a seat belt. The police have to issue a receipt for the amount paid.

SOME COMMON ROAD SIGNS

The majority of road signs in France follow international conventions, but you may see the following:

accotement non stabilisé	soft verge
aire de croisement	passing place
arrêt interdit	no stopping
autoroute	motorway
autoroute à péage	toll motorway
autres directions	other directions
brouillard fréquent	risk of fog
carrefour dangereux	dangerous crossroads

➜

centre-ville	town centre
chaussée déformée	uneven road surface
chaussée glissante	slippery road surface
chute de pierres	falling rocks
danger de verglas	danger of black ice
déviation	diversion
douane	customs
école	school
embranchement d'autoroutes	motorway junction
entrée interdite	no entry
fin d'autoroute	end of motorway
gravillons	loose chippings
I	tourist information
nids-de-poule	potholes
passage à niveau	level crossing
passage interdit	no thoroughfare
passage protégé	priority road
péage	toll
piétons	pedestrians
poids lourds	heavy vehicles
point noir	accident blackspot
premiers secours	first aid
prudence	caution
ralentir	slow down
rappel	reminder
riverains autorisés	residents only
route barrée	road closed
route départementale	secondary road
route nationale	main road
route verglacée	black ice
sens unique	one-way street
serrez à droite	keep to the right
stationnement à durée limitée	restricted parking
stationnement alterné	parking on alternate sides
stationnement interdit	no parking
toutes directions	all directions →

travaux	roadworks	
virage dangereux	dangerous bend	
virages sur ... km	bends for ... km	
voie pour véhicules lents	crawler lane	
zone piétonnière	pedestrian precinct	

USEFUL WORDS AND PHRASES

automatic	automatique	*ohtomateek*
bonnet	le capot	*kapoh*
boot	le coffre	*koffr*
brakes	les freins	*frAN*
car	la voiture	*vwahtOOr*
car ferry	le car ferry	*kar fairree*
car park	le parking	*par-keeng*
(multistorey)	le parking à étages	*par-keeng ah aytaĴ*
clutch	l'embrayage	*ONbrayaĴ*
crossroads	le carrefour	*karrfoor*
drive	conduire	*kONdweer*
engine	le moteur	*motur*
exhaust	le pot d'échappement	*poh dayshappmON*
fanbelt	la courroie du ventilateur	*koo-rwah dOO vONteelatur*
garage *(for repairs)*	le garage	*garraĴ*
(for petrol)	la station-service	*stass-iON sairveess*
gear	la vitesse	*veetess*
gear box	la boîte de vitesses	*bwat duh veetess*
headlights	les phares	*far*
indicator	le clignotant	*kleen-yotON*
junction	le croisement	*krwahzmON*
(motorway entry)	l'entrée	*ONtray*
(motorway exit)	la sortie	*sortee*
licence	le permis de conduire	*permee duh kONdweer*
lorry	le camion	*kamiON*

manual	manuelle	*manOO-el*
mirror	le rétroviseur	*raytroveezur*
motorbike	la moto	*motoh*
motorway	l'autoroute	*ohto-root*
number plate	la plaque d'immatriculation	*plak deematreekOO-lass-iON*
petrol	l'essence	*essONss*
petrol station	la station-service	*stass-iON sairveess*
rear lights	les feux arrière	*fuh arree-air*
road	la route	*root*
skid	déraper	*dayrappay*
spares	des pièces de rechange	*pee-ess duh ruhshONJ*
spark plug	la bougie	*booJee*
speed	la vitesse	*veetess*
speed limit	vitesse limitée	*veetess leemeetay*
speedometer	le compteur de vitesse	*kONtur duh veetess*
steering wheel	le volant	*volON*
traffic lights	les feux	*fuh*
trailer	la remorque	*ruhmork*
tyre	le pneu	*p-nuh*
van	la camionnette	*kamionet*
vehicle registration documents	la carte grise	*kart greez*
wheel	la roue	*roo*
windscreen	le pare-brise	*par breez*
windscreen wiper	un essuie-glace	*esswee glass*

I'd like some petrol/oil/water
Je voudrais de l'essence/de l'huile/de l'eau
Juh voodreh duh lessONss/duh lweel/duh loh

Fill her up please!
Le plein, s'il vous plaît !
luh plAN seel voo pleh

I'd like 35 litres of 4-star
Je voudrais trente-cinq litres de super
Juh voodreh trONt sANk leetr duh sOOpair

Do you do repairs?
Faites-vous les réparations ?
fet voo lay rayparass-iON

Can you repair the clutch?
Pouvez-vous réparer l'embrayage ?
poovay voo rayparay lONbrayaJ

How long will it take?
Combien de temps est-ce que ça prendra ?
kONbyAN duh tON esskuh sa prONdra

Can you repair it today?
Pouvez-vous le réparer aujourd'hui ?
poovay voo luh rayparay ohJoordwee

There is something wrong with the engine
Le moteur ne fonctionne pas bien
luh motur nuh fONkss-iON pa byAN

The engine is overheating
Le moteur chauffe
luh motur shohf

I need a new tyre
Je voudrais un pneu neuf
Juh voodreh AN p-nuh nuhf

Can you replace this?
Pouvez-vous remplacer ceci ?
poovay voo rONplassay suhsee

The indicator is not working
Le clignotant ne fonctionne pas
luh kleen-yotON nuh fONkss-iON pa

42

Is there a car park near here?
Est-ce qu'il y a un parking dans les environs ?
esskeel-ya AN par-keeng dON layz ONveerON

Can I park here?
Est-ce que je peux me garer ici ?
esskuh Juh puh muh garray ee-see

Do I have to pay?
Faut-il payer ?
fohteel payay

I'd like to hire a car
Je voudrais louer une voiture
Juh voodreh loo-ay OOn vwahtOOr

I'd like an automatic/a manual
J'aimerais une voiture à transmission automatique/manuelle
*Jemmereh OOn vwahtOOr ah trONsmeess-iON ohtomateek/
manOO-el*

How much is it for one day?
Ça coûte combien pour une journée?
sa koot kONbyAN poor OOn Joornay

Is there a mileage charge?
Est-ce qu'il y a des frais de kilométrage ?
esskeel-ya day freh duh keelomaytraJ

When do I have to return it?
Quand est-ce que je dois la ramener ?
kONt esskuh Juh dwah la ramuhnay

Where is the nearest garage?
Pouvez-vous m'indiquer le garage le plus proche ?
poovay voo mANdeekay luh garraJ luh ploo prosh

How do I get to ...?
Comment va-t-on à ... ?
kommON vat ON ah

Is this the road to …?
Est-ce que c'est bien la route pour … ?
esskuh seh byAN la root poor

Which is the quickest way to …?
Quelle est la voie la plus rapide pour arriver à … ?
kell eh la vwah la plOO rapeed poor arreevay ah

DIRECTIONS YOU MAY BE GIVEN

à droite	right
à gauche	left
au prochain carrefour	at the next crossroads
avancez	go forward
deuxième à gauche	second on the left
passez …	go past …
première à droite	first on the right
reculez	reverse
tournez à droite/gauche	turn right/left
tout droit	straight on

THINGS YOU'LL SEE

aire de repos	rest area
aire de service	service area
aire de stationnement	parking area
arrêtez votre moteur	switch off engine
attendez ici	wait here
cire pour voiture	car wax
eau	water
essence	petrol
gas-oil	diesel
horodateur	pay and display
huile	oil

→

lavage du pare-brise	screen wash
montant exact	exact change
ordinaire	equivalent of two-star petrol
parcmètre	parking meter
parking	car park
parking à étages	multistorey car park
parking payant	paying car park
parking surveillé	car park with attendant
prenez un ticket	take a ticket
pression de l'air	air pressure
pression des pneus	tyre pressure
réparations	repairs
réservé aux clients	patrons only
roulez au pas	drive at walking pace
sans plomb	lead-free
sortie	exit
station-service	petrol station
super	four-star petrol

THINGS YOU'LL HEAR

Voulez-vous une voiture à transmission automatique ou à transmission manuelle ?
Would you like an automatic or a manual?

Puis-je voir votre permis de conduire ?
May I see your licence?

Puis-je voir votre passeport ?
May I see your passport?

TRAVELLING AROUND

AIR TRAVEL

Paris has two international airports, Orly and Charles de Gaulle at Roissy. Both are connected to the main terminals and railway stations in Paris by **navettes** (airport buses). There's also a train service to Charles de Gaulle, the fast **RER**, which connects with a free shuttle bus to the air terminal.

FERRY, HOVERCRAFT AND BOAT TRAVEL

Many companies run car ferry and hovercraft services across the Channel and there are also car ferries to Corsica from Marseilles, Toulon and Nice.

There are many opportunities for boat trips and self-drive cruises on the rivers and canals of France, including areas such as Burgundy, Brittany and Alsace among others.

RAIL TRAVEL

The French railways (**SNCF**) are both fast and punctual, and have two classes, first and second. International trains connect Paris with most parts of Europe, while fast, regular Inter-City and express services link the main French towns. The main types of train are:

TGV (Train à Grande Vitesse): High-speed train.

Rapide: fast Inter-City train, often named (l'Aquitaine, le Drapeau, l'Etendard, le Mistral etc).

Express: an ordinary fast train.

You may see the sign **supplément modulé**, which means that you have to pay a supplement if travelling on a Friday or the day before a public holiday. Booking is essential on the **TGV** train and it is compulsory to buy **une résa** (reservation ticket) with your ticket, both of which you must date-stamp on the day of use. Look for a machine with the sign **compostez votre billet** (stamp your ticket). If you buy any rail ticket in France (rather than book it before you get there), you must validate this by inserting it into one of the orange-coloured machines at the platform entrance. If you don't date-stamp it like this, you may be fined by a roving ticket inspector.

BUS

In the country, buses link mainline railway stations with most towns and villages not served by trains. Tickets are available at **tabac-journaux** (newsagents) and – as in Paris, where the same tickets or passes can be used either on the **métro** or on the bus – fares are calculated by distance, one ticket for one fare stage. You must date-stamp your ticket in the machine on the bus – you will see the sign: **oblitérez votre ticket** (punch your ticket). Long-distance coach services are rare in France but there are sightseeing package tours by coach.

UNDERGROUND AND SUBURBAN TRAINS

In Paris, the **métro** (underground) is the fastest and most economical way to travel. It's a one-price service regardless of distance, and trains run from about 5.30 am to 12.30 am. Tickets are cheapest when bought in booklets of ten (**carnet**), and you can also buy special tourist tickets (enquire at **métro** or railway stations, or at any Office de Tourisme in Paris). Lille, Lyons and Marseilles also have **métro** systems.

There is an extensive suburban train network in Paris – **RER** (**Réseau Express Régional**) – operated jointly by the **SNCF** and Paris transport.

TAXI

Taxis are clearly marked and can be hailed or picked up at a rank (there's usually one at the train station). If the cab has no meter, or if you are going some distance out of town, check the fare beforehand.

USEFUL WORDS AND PHRASES

adult	un adulte	*adOOlt*
airport	l'aéroport	*ah-ayropor*
airport bus	la navette de l'aéroport	*navet duh lah-ayropor*
aisle seat	une place côté couloir	*plass kohtay koolwahr*
baggage claim	le retrait des bagages	*ruhtray day bagaJ*
boarding card	la carte d'embarquement	*kart dONbarkuhmON*
boat	le bateau	*battoh*
booking office	le guichet	*gheeshay*
buffet	le buffet de la gare	*bOOfay duh la gar*
bus	le bus	*bOOss*
bus station	la gare routière	*gar rootee-air*
bus stop	un arrêt de bus	*array duh bOOss*
check-in desk	l'enregistrement des bagages	*ONruhJeestruh-mON day bagaJ*
child	un enfant	*ONfON*
coach *(bus)*	un car	*kar*
compartment	le compartiment	*kONparteemON*
connection	la correspondance	*korrespON-dONss*
cruise	la croisière	*krwahzee-air*
Customs	la douane	*doo-wan*
departure lounge	la salle d'embarquement	*sal dONbarkmON*
domestic arrivals	arrivées intérieures	*arreevay ANtayree-ur*
domestic departures	départs intérieurs	*daypar ANtayree-ur*
entrance	l'entrée	*ONtray*
excess baggage	l'excédent de bagages	*eksaidON duh bagaJ*
exit	la sortie	*sortee*
fare	le prix du ticket	*pree dOO teekay*
ferry	le ferry	*fairree*
first class	première classe	*pruhmee-air klass*
flight	le vol	*vol*

flight number	le numéro du vol	*nOOmayroh dOO vol*
gate	la porte	*port*
hand luggage	les bagages à main	*bagaʒ ah mAN*
hovercraft	un hovercraft,	*ovairkraft,*
	un aéroglisseur	*ah-ayrohgleesur*
hoverport	un hoverport	*ovairpor*
hydrofoil	un hydrofoil,	*eedro-foyl,*
	un hydroptère	*eedroptair*
international arrivals	arrivées internationales	*arreevay ANtairnass-ionahl*
international departures	départs internationaux	*daypar ANtairnass-ionoh*
left-luggage office	la consigne	*konseen*
lost property office	le bureau des objets trouvés	*bOOroh dayz obʒay troovay*
luggage trolley	un chariot	*sharee-oh*
network map	un plan du réseau	*plON dOO rayzoh*
non-smoking	non-fumeurs	*nON fOOmur*
number 5 bus	le bus numéro 5	*bOOss nOOmayroh sANk*
passport	un passeport	*passpor*
platform	le quai	*kay*
port	le port	*por*
railway	le chemin de fer	*shuhmAN duh fair*
restaurant car	le wagon-restaurant	*vagON restorON*
return ticket	un aller retour	*allay-ruhtoor*
seat	une place	*plass*
second class	seconde	*segONd*
subway	un passage souterrain	*passaʒ sootairrAN*
single ticket	un aller simple	*allay sANp-l*
sleeper	un wagon-lit	*vagON lee*
smoking	fumeurs	*fOOmur*
station	la gare	*gar*
(underground)	la station	*stass-iON*
taxi	un taxi	*taxee*
terminus	le terminus	*tairmeenOOs*

49

ticket *(air, rail)*	un billet	*bee-yay*
(bus, métro)	un ticket	*teekay*
timetable	l'horaire	*orrair*
train	le train	*trAN*
underground	le métro	*maytroh*
waiting room	la salle d'attente	*sal dattONt*
window seat *(air)*	une place côté hublot	*plass kohtay OObloh*
(rail)	une place côté fenêtre	*plass kohtay fuhn-ettr*

AIR TRAVEL

I'd like a non-smoking seat please
Je voudrais une place en non-fumeurs, s'il vous plaît
Juh voodreh OOn plass ON nON fOOmur seel voo pleh

I'd like a window seat please
Je voudrais une place côté hublot, s'il vous plaît
Juh voodreh OOn plass kohtay OObloh seel voo pleh

How long will the flight be delayed?
Combien l'avion aura-t-il de retard ?
kONbyAN lav-iON oh-ratteel duh ruhtar

Which gate for the flight to London?
Quelle porte pour le vol à destination de Londres ?
kell port poor luh vol ah desteenass-ion duh lONdr

TRAIN, BUS AND UNDERGROUND TRAVEL

When does the train/bus for Paris leave/arrive?
A quelle heure part/arrive le train/bus pour Paris ?
ah kell ur par/arreev luh trAN/bOOss poor paree

When is the next train/bus to Lyons?
A quelle heure part le prochain train/bus pour Lyon ?
ah kell ur par luh proshAN trAN/bOOss poor lee-on

When is the first/last train/bus to Grenoble?
A quelle heure part le premier/dernier train/bus pour Grenoble ?
ah kell ur par luh pruhm-yay/dairn-yay trAN/bOOss poor gruhnob-l

What is the fare to Nantes?
Quelle est le prix du billet pour Nantes ?
kell eh luh pree dOO bee-yay poor nONt

Do I have to change trains/buses?
Faut-il que je change de train/bus ?
foh-teel kuh Juh shONj duh trAN/bOOss

Does the train/bus stop at Rouen?
Est-ce que le train/bus s'arrête à Rouen ?
esskuh luh trAN/bOOss sarret ah roo-ON

How long does it take to get to Bordeaux?
Combien de temps faut-il pour aller à Bordeaux ?
kONbyAN duh tON foh-teel poor allay ah bordoh

Where can I buy a ticket?
Où est-ce que je peux acheter un billet ?
oo esskuh Juh puh ashtay AN bee-yay

A single/return ticket to Strasbourg please
Un aller simple/aller retour Strasbourg, s'il vous plaît
AN allay sANp-l/allay-ruhtoor strazboorg seel voo pleh

Could you help me get a ticket?
Pouvez-vous m'aider à obtenir un billet ?
poovay voo mayday ah obtuhneer AN bee-yay

Do I have to pay a supplement?
Est-ce qu'il y a un supplément à payer ?
esskeel-ya AN sOOplaymON ah pay-ay

I'd like to reserve a seat
Je voudrais réserver une place
Juh voodreh rayzairvay OOn plass

Is this the right train/bus for Montpellier?
Est-ce bien le train/bus pour Montpellier ?
ess byAN luh trAN/bOOss poor mONpailee-yay

Is this the right platform for the Nice train?
Est-ce bien le quai pour le train qui va à Nice ?
ess byAN le kay poor luh trAN kee va ah neess

Which platform for the Lille train?
De quel quai part le train pour Lille ?
duh kell kay par luh trAN poor leel

Is the train/bus late?
Est-ce que le train/bus a du retard ?
esskuh luh trAN/bOOss ah dOO ruhtar

Is this a non-smoking compartment?
Ce compartiment est-il non-fumeurs ?
suh kONpartee-mON eteel nON fOOmur

Is this seat free?
Est-ce que cette place est libre ?
esskuh set plass eh leebr

This seat is taken
Cette place est occupée
set plass et okkOOpay

I have reserved this seat
J'ai réservé cette place
Jay rayzairvay set plass

May I open/close the window?
Est-ce que je peux ouvrir/fermer la fenêtre ?
esskuh Juh puh oovreer/fairmay la fuhn-ettr

When do we arrive in Toulouse?
Savez-vous à quelle heure nous arriverons à Toulouse ?
savay voo ah kell ur nooz arreevuhrON ah toolooz

What station is this?
Quelle est cette gare ?
kell eh set gar

Do we stop at Metz?
Est-ce que le train/bus s'arrête à Metz ?
esskuh luh trAN/bOOss sarret ah metz

Would you keep an eye on my things for a moment?
Pouvez-vous surveiller mes affaires pendant un moment ?
poovay voo sOOrvay-yay mayz affair pONdON AN momON

Is there a restaurant car on this train?
Est-ce qu'il y a un wagon-restaurant dans ce train ?
esskeel-ya AN vagON restorON dON suh trAN

REPLIES YOU MAY BE GIVEN

Le prochain train part à ...
The next train leaves at ...

Changez à ...
Change at ...

Vous devez payer un supplément
You must pay a supplement

Il n'y a plus de places disponibles pour ...
There are no more seats available on ...

Where is the nearest underground station?
Pouvez-vous m'indiquer la station de métro la plus proche ?
poovay voo mANdeekay la stass-iON duh maytroh la plOO prosh

Which buses go to the city centre?
Quels sont les bus qui vont au centre-ville ?
kell sON lay bOOss kee vON oh sONtr veel

How often do the buses to Bourg-en-Bresse run?
Quelle est la fréquence des bus pour Bourg-en-Bresse ?
kell eh la fraykONss day bOOss poor boorg-ON-bress

Will you let me know when we're there?
Pourriez-vous me faire savoir quand nous y serons ?
pooree-ay voo muh fair savvwahr kON nooz ee suhrON

Do I have to get off yet?
Faut-il que je descende maintenant ?
foh-teel kuh Juh daysONd mANtnON

Do you go near the Musée d'Orsay?
Passez-vous près du Musée d'Orsay ?
passay voo preh dOO mOOzay dorsay

TAXI

Can you let me off here?
Pouvez-vous me déposer ici ?
poovay voo muh daypozay ee-see

How much is it to the station?
Combien ça coûte pour aller à la gare ?
kONbyAN sa koot poor allay ah la gar

Could you wait here for me and take me back?
Pourriez-vous m'attendre ici et me ramener ?
pooree-ay voo mattONdr ee-see ay muh ramuhnay

THINGS YOU'LL SEE

accès aux quais/trains	to the platforms/trains
aérogare	air terminal
aéroglisseur	hovercraft
annuler	cancel

appuyez ici	press here
arrêt de bus	bus stop
arrêt facultatif	request stop
arrivée(s)	arrival(s)
banlieue	suburbs
billeterie automatique	ticket machine
billets	tickets
carnet	book of tickets
carte	pass
carte de réduction	pass enabling you to buy a reduced-rate rail ticket
cet appareil ne rend pas la monnaie	this machine does not give change
change	currency exchange
compostez votre billet	stamp your ticket
consigne	left luggage
consigne automatique	luggage lockers
contrôle des bagages	luggage control
cordon d'alarme	emergency cord
correspondance	transfers, connection
dames	ladies (toilet)
départ(s)	departure(s)
dessert …	stops at …
dimanches et jours fériés	on Sundays and public holidays
douane	Customs
embarquement	boarding
enfants	children
entrée	entrance
entrée à l'avant/à l'arrière	entry at the front/rear
entrée interdite	no entry
Express	ordinary fast train
fermeture automatique des portes	doors close automatically
fumeurs	smoking
gare	station

→

grandes lignes	main lines
guichet	ticket office
heure	time
hommes	gents (toilet)
horaire	timetable
hydroptère	hydrofoil
interdit aux voyageurs	staff only
introduire ici	insert here
issue de secours	emergency exit
journées à tarif réduit	cheap travel days
jours de semaine uniquement	weekdays only
libre	vacant
livraison des bagages	baggage claim
navette de l'aéroport	airport bus
ne pas se pencher par la fenêtre	do not lean out of the window
non-fumeurs	no smoking
n'oubliez pas de composter votre billet	don't forget to validate your ticket
oblitérez votre billet	punch your ticket
occupé	engaged
ouverture	opening
passage interdit	no entry
passager(s)	passenger(s)
passage souterrain	subway
payez ici	pay here
pénalité pour abus	penalty for misuse
pièce(s)	coin(s)
pièces rejetées	reject coins
place (assise)	seat
plan de métro	underground map
plan du réseau	network map
plein tarif	full price
porte	gate

→

pour faire votre choix, appuyez sur l'écran	to make your selection, touch the screen
poussez	push
quai	platform; quay
rame	train
Rapide	inter-city train
relevez	lift up
renseignements	enquiries
RER	Paris suburban rail network
résa	reservation ticket on TGV
réservé	reserved
réservé au personnel	staff only
retard/retardé	delay/delayed
salle d'attente	waiting room
sans issue	no way out
satellite	section of airport terminal
SNCF	French Railways
sortie	exit
sortie de secours	emergency exit
station de métro	underground station
station de taxis	taxi rank
tabac-journaux	newspaper kiosk
TGV	high-speed train
ticket de quai	platform ticket
ticket ou carnet de métro	métro ticket or book of tickets
tirez	pull
titre de transport	ticket
tous les jours sauf ...	every day except ...
train à supplément	train for which you must pay a supplement
voie	platform, track
voiture	coach, car
vol direct	direct flight
vols intérieurs	domestic flights
wagon-lit	sleeper

THINGS YOU'LL HEAR

Avez-vous des bagages ?
Have you any luggage?

Fumeurs ou non-fumeurs ?
Smoking or non-smoking?

Place côté hublot ou côté couloir ?
Window seat or aisle seat?

Prière de vous rendre maintenant à la porte numéro quatre
Please proceed to gate number four

Les billets, s'il vous plaît
Tickets please

Attention au départ
The train is about to leave

Le train à destination de Paris partira de la voie 4 dans 10 minutes
The train for Paris will leave from platform 4 in 10 minutes

Le train en provenance de Rennes arrivera à la voie 5 dans 15 minutes
The train from Rennes will arrive at platform 5 in 15 minutes

Le train en provenance de Bordeaux a un retard de 17 minutes
The train from Bordeaux is running 17 minutes late

Préparez vos billets, s'il vous plaît
Have your tickets ready, please

Ouvrez vos valises, s'il vous plaît
Open your suitcases, please

RESTAURANTS

It is not difficult to eat well and at little cost in France. Since prices have by law to be displayed in the window of an eating establishment, you can readily fit your choice of restaurant to your budget. Although service is included in the bill, it is customary to leave a tip for the waiter or waitress. In cafés, even if you have just popped in for a coffee or drink, it is traditional to leave the odd coins from your change.

Every town has a number of cafés where at lunch time you can order a simple sandwich, a **croque-monsieur** (a grilled ham and cheese sandwich which, with the addition of an egg, becomes a **croque-madame**), the **plat du jour** (dish of the day), **rillettes** (pork or goose meat minced very finely so that it can be spread on bread), pâté or a platter of crudités or cold meats.

Bistros are small bars, often family-run, which also sometimes serve a selection of traditional dishes or snacks at lunch time and in the evening. The **menu du jour** (today's menu) is usually extremely good value. Regional specialities that you may encounter include: **crêpes** in Brittany; **choucroute** (sauerkraut with sausages and pieces of smoked ham) and onion tart in Alsace; **ratatouille** in Provence; and **bouillabaisse** (fish soup) and **salade niçoise** (mixed salad containing olives, anchovies, tuna, tomatoes and other vegetables) around the Mediterranean coast. House wine is available in carafes but if you prefer your wine by the bottle, you will find a few listed on the menu.

Brasseries are often large and noisy – not the place to go for an intimate dinner – and offer beer on tap as well as wine. They stay open late and snacks and full meals are usually available at any time.

If you are planning a picnic, **charcuteries** offer a very wide range of take-away food, such as sausages, pâté, ham, quiche and a wide range of salads. Some of the items on offer that may not be readily identifiable are: **andouille** (a cold sausage made from pig's or calf's intestines); **boudin blanc** (white pudding); **crépinette** (a small sausage patty wrapped in fat); **fromage de**

tête (brawn); **poitrine fumée** (smoked bacon), and **rillettes** The difference between a **saucisse** and a **saucisson**, by the way. is that the former is fresh and eaten warm, the latter dried and eaten cold.

French cafés and bars always sell coffee, unlike their English counterparts. If you ask for **un café** or **un express**, you'll get a small, black coffee. **Un crème** is a small coffee with milk and **un grand crème** is a large coffee with milk. You can also ask for **un café léger** (weak coffee) or **un café bien serré** (very strong coffee).

USEFUL WORDS AND PHRASES

beer	de la bière	*bee-air*
bill	l'addition	*addeess-iON*
bottle	une bouteille	*bootay*
bread	du pain	*pAN*
butter	du beurre	*bur*
café	un café	*kaffay*
cake	du gâteau	*gattoh*
carafe	une carafe	*karaff*
chef	le chef	*shef*
children's portion	une portion enfant	*porss-iON ONfON*
coffee	du café	*kaffay*
cup	une tasse	*tass*
dessert	un dessert	*daissair*
fork	une fourchette	*foorshet*
glass	un verre	*vair*
half-litre	un demi-litre	*duhmee leettr*
knife	un couteau	*kootoh*
main course	le plat principal	*pla prANseepal*
menu	le menu	*muhnOO*
milk	du lait	*leh*
pepper	du poivre	*pwahvr*
plate	une assiette	*assee-et*
receipt	le reçu	*ruhssOO*

60

restaurant	le restaurant	*restohrON*
salt	du sel	*sel*
sandwich	un sandwich	*sONdweech*
serviette	une serviette	*sairvee-et*
snack	un snack	*'snack'*
soup	de la soupe	*soop*
spoon	une cuillère	*kwee-air*
starter	une entrée	*ONtray*
sugar	du sucre	*sOOkr*
table	une table	*tabb-l*
tea	du thé	*tay*
teaspoon	une cuillère à café	*kwee-air ah kaffay*
tip	un pourboire	*poorbwahr*
waiter	un serveur	*sairvur*
waitress	une serveuse	*sairvuhz*
water	de l'eau	*oh*
wine	du vin	*vAN*
wine list	la carte des vins	*kart day vAN*

A table for one please
Une table pour une personne, s'il vous plaît
OOn tabb-l poor OOn pairson seel voo pleh

A table for two/three please
Une table pour deux/trois personnes, s'il vous plaît
OOn tabb-l poor duh/trwah pairson seel voo pleh

Can we see the menu/wine list?
Le menu/la carte des vins, s'il vous plaît
luh muhnOO/la kart day vAN seel voo pleh

What would you recommend?
Que recommandez-vous ?
kuh ruhkommONday voo

I'd like ...
J'aimerais ...
Jemmereh

Just a cup of coffee/tea, please
Un café/thé seulement
AN kaffay/tay suhlmON

I only want a snack
Je voudrais juste manger un snack
Juh voodreh JOOst mONJay AN 'snack'

Is there a set menu?
Est-ce qu'il y a un menu du jour ?
esskeel-ya AN muhnOO dOO joor

A carafe of house red, please
Une carafe de vin rouge maison, s'il vous plaît
OOn karaff duh vAN rooJ mezzON seel voo pleh

Do you have any vegetarian dishes?
Est-ce que vous servez des plats végétariens ?
esskuh voo sairvay day pla vayJaytaryAN

Could we have some water?
Est-ce que nous pourrions avoir de l'eau ?
esskuh noo pooree-ON avwahr duh loh

Do you do children's portions?
Est-ce que vous servez des portions enfant ?
esskuh voo sairvay day porss-iON ONfON

Waiter/waitress!
Garçon/Mademoiselle !
garssON/madmwazel

We didn't order this
Ce n'est pas ce que nous avons commandé
sneh pa suh kuh nooz avON kommONday

You've forgotten to bring my dessert
Vous avez oublié d'apporter mon dessert
vooz avay ooblee-ay dapportay mON daissair

May we have some more ...?
Est-ce qu'on peut avoir plus de ... ?
esskON puh avwahr plOO duh

Can I have another knife/fork ?
Est-ce que je peux avoir un autre couteau/une autre fourchette ?
esskuh Juh puh avwahr AN oht-r kootoh/OOn oht-r foorshet

Can we have the bill, please?
L'addition, s'il vous plaît !
laddeess-iON seel voo pleh

Could I have a receipt, please?
Est-ce que je peux avoir un reçu, s'il vous plaît ?
esskuh Juh puh avwahr AN ruhssOO seel voo pleh

Can we pay separately?
Est-ce que nous pouvons payer séparément ?
esskuh noo poovON pay-ay sayparaymON

The meal was very good, thank you
C'était très bon, merci
sayteh treh bON mairsee

My compliments to the chef!
Complimentez le chef de ma part !
kompleemONtay luh shef duh ma par

YOU MAY HEAR

Bon appétit !
Enjoy your meal!

Que désirez-vous boire ?
What would you like to drink?

MENU GUIDE

abats	offal
abricot	apricot
à emporter	to take away
agneau	lamb
aiguillette de bœuf	slices of rump steak
ail	garlic
ailloli	garlic mayonnaise
à la broche	roasted on a spit
à la jardinière	with assorted vegetables
à la normande	in cream sauce
alose	shad *(fish)*
amande	almond
ananas	pineapple
anchois	anchovies
andouillette	spicy sausage
anguille	eel
à point	well done
araignée de mer	spider crab
artichaut	artichoke
asperge	asparagus
aspic de volaille	chicken in aspic
assiette anglaise	selection of cold meats
au gratin	baked in a milk, cream and cheese sauce
au vin blanc	in white wine
avocat	avocado
baba au rhum	rum baba
banane	banana
bananes flambées	bananas flambéd in brandy
barbue	brill *(fish)*
bavaroise	light mousse
béarnaise	with *béarnaise* sauce (thick sauce made with eggs and butter)
bécasse	woodcock
béchamel	white sauce, *béchamel* sauce
beignet	fritter, doughnut
beignet aux pommes	apple fritter
betterave	beetroot
beurre	butter

beurre d'anchois	anchovy paste
beurre d'estragon	butter with tarragon
beurre noir	dark melted butter
bien cuit	well done
bière	beer
bière à la pression	draught beer
bière blonde	lager
bière brune	bitter, dark beer
bière panachée	shandy
bifteck	steak
bifteck de cheval	horsemeat steak
biscuit de Savoie	sponge cake
bisque d'écrevisses	crayfish soup
bisque de homard	lobster soup
blanc de blancs	white wine from white grapes
blanquette de veau	veal stew
bleu	rare
bleu d'auvergne	blue cheese from Auvergne
bœuf	beef
bœuf à la ficelle	beef cooked in stock
bœuf bourguignon	beef cooked in red wine
bœuf braisé	braised beef
bœuf en daube	beef casserole
bœuf miroton	beef and onion stew
bœuf mode	beef stew with carrots
bolet	boletus *(mushroom)*
bouchée à la reine	chicken vol-au-vent
boudin blanc	white pudding
boudin noir	black pudding
bouillabaisse	fish soup from the Midi
bouilli	boiled
bouillon	broth
bouillon de légumes	vegetable stock
bouillon de poule	chicken stock
boulette	meatball
bouquet rose	prawns
bourride	fish soup
braisé	braised
brandade	cod in cream and garlic
brioche	round bun
brochet	pike
brochette	kebab

brugnon	nectarine
brûlot	flambéd brandy
brut	very dry
cabillaud	cod
café	coffee *(black)*
café au lait	white coffee
café complet	continental breakfast
café crème	white coffee
café glacé	iced coffee
café liégeois	iced coffee with cream
caille	quail
cake	fruit cake
calamar/calmar	squid
calvados	apple brandy
camomille	camomile tea
canapé	small open sandwich, canapé
canard	duck
canard à l'orange	duck in orange sauce
canard aux cerises	duck with cherries
canard aux navets	duck with turnips
canard laqué	Pekin duck
canard rôti	roast duck
caneton	duckling
cantal	cheese from Auvergne
carbonnade	beef cooked in beer
cari	curry
carotte	carrot
carottes Vichy	carrots in butter and parsley
carpe	carp
carré d'agneau	rack of lamb
carrelet	plaice
carte	menu
carte des vins	wine list
casse-croûte	snacks
cassis	blackcurrant
cassoulet	bean, pork and duck casserole
céleri	celeriac
céleri en branches	celery
céleri rave	celeriac
céleri rémoulade	celeriac in *rémoulade* dressing
cèpe	cep *(mushroom)*
cerise	cherry

cerises à l'eau de vie	cherries in brandy
cervelle	brains
chabichou	goat's and cow's milk cheese
chablis	dry white wine from Burgundy
chambré	at room temperature
champignon	mushroom
champignon de Paris	white button mushroom
champignons à la grecque	dish of mushrooms in olive oil, herbs and tomatoes, served hot or cold
chanterelle	chanterelle *(mushroom)*
chantilly	whipped cream
charcuterie	sausages, ham and pâtés, pork products
charlotte	dessert consisting of layers of fruit, cream and biscuits
chasselas	white grape
chausson aux pommes	apple turnover
cheval	horse
chèvre	goat's cheese
chevreuil	venison
chicorée	endive
chiffonnade d'oseille	seasoned sorrel cooked in butter
chocolat chaud	hot chocolate
chocolat glacé	iced chocolate
chocolatine	chocolate puff pastry
chou	cabbage
chou à la crème	cream puff
choucroute	sauerkraut with sausages and pieces of smoked ham
chou-fleur	cauliflower
chou-fleur au gratin	cauliflower cheese
chou rouge	red cabbage
choux de Bruxelles	Brussels sprouts
cidre	cider
cidre doux	sweet cider
citron	lemon
citron pressé	fresh lemon juice
civet de lièvre	jugged hare
clafoutis	baked batter pudding with fruit
cochon de lait	sucking pig
cocktail de crevettes	prawn cocktail
cœur	heart

coing	quince
colin	hake
compote	stewed fruit, compote
comté	hard cheese from the Jura
concombre	cucumber
confit de canard	duck preserved in fat
confit d'oie	goose preserved in fat
confiture	jam
congre	conger eel
consommé	clear soup made from meat or chicken
coq au vin	chicken in red wine
coque	cockle
coquelet	cockerel
coquille Saint-Jacques	scallop served in cream sauce
côte de porc	pork chop
côtelette	chop
cotriade bretonne	fish soup from Brittany
coulommiers	rich, soft cheese
coupe	dessert dish
court-bouillon	stock for poaching fish or meat
couscous	steamed grains of semolina with meat and vegetable stew
crabe	crab
crème	cream, creamy sauce or dessert; white coffee
crème à la vanille	vanilla custard
crème anglaise	custard
crème chantilly	whipped cream
crème d'asperges	cream of asparagus soup
crème de bolets	cream of mushroom soup
crème de volaille	cream of chicken soup
crème d'huîtres	cream of oyster soup
crème fouettée	whipped cream
crème pâtissière	rich creamy custard
crème renversée	set custard
crème vichyssoise	cold potato and leek soup
crêpe	pancake
crêpe à la béchamel	pancake with *béchamel* sauce
crêpe à la chantilly	pancake with whipped cream
crêpe à la confiture	pancake with jam
crêpe à la crème de marron	pancake with chestnut cream
crêpe à l'œuf	pancake with fried egg

crêpe au chocolat	pancake with chocolate sauce
crêpe au jambon	pancake with ham
crêpe aux fruits de mer	pancake with seafood
crêpe de froment	wholemeal pancake
crêpes aux champignons	mushroom pancakes
crêpes aux épinards	spinach pancakes
crêpes Suzette	pancakes flambéd with orange sauce
crépinette	small sausage patty wrapped in fat
cresson	cress
crevette grise	shrimp
crevette rose	prawn
croque-madame	toasted cheese and ham sandwich with a fried egg
croque-monsieur	toasted cheese and ham sandwich
crottin de Chavignol	small goat's cheese
crudités	selection of salads, chopped raw vegetables
crustacés	shellfish
cuisses de grenouille	frogs' legs
cuissot de chevreuil	haunch of venison
dartois	pastry with jam
daurade	gilt-head *(fish)*
dégustation	(wine) tasting
déjeuner	lunch
digestif	liqueur
dinde	turkey
dîner	dinner
doux	sweet
eau minérale	mineral water
eau minérale gazeuse	sparkling mineral water
échalote	shallot
écrevisse	saltwater crayfish
écrevisses à la nage	crayfish in wine and vegetable sauce
endive	chicory, endive
endives au jambon	endives with ham baked in the oven
en papillote	baked in foil or paper
entrecôte	rib steak
entrecôte au poivre	peppered rib steak
entrecôte maître d'hôtel	steak with butter and parsley
entrée	starter
entremets	dessert
épaule d'agneau farcie	stuffed shoulder of lamb

éperlan	smelt *(fish)*
épinards à la crème	spinach with cream
épinards en branches	leaf spinach
escalope à la crème	escalope in cream sauce
escalope de veau milanaise	veal escalope with tomato sauce
escalope panée	breaded escalope
escargot	snail
esquimau	ice cream on a stick
estouffade de bœuf	beef casserole
faisan	pheasant
farci	stuffed
fenouil	fennel
filet	fillet
filet de bœuf Rossini	fillet of beef with *foie gras*
filet de perche	perch fillet
fine	fine brandy
flageolets	kidney beans
flambé	flambéd
flan	custard tart
foie de veau	veal liver
foie gras	goose or duck liver preserve
foies de volaille	chicken livers
fonds d'artichaut	artichoke hearts
fondue bourguignonne	meat fondue
fondue savoyarde	cheese fondue
fraise	strawberry
fraise des bois	wild strawberry
framboise	raspberry
frisée	curly lettuce
frit	deep-fried
frites	chips, French fries
fromage	cheese
fromage blanc	cream cheese
fromage de chèvre	goat's cheese
fruité	fruity
fruits de mer	seafood
galette	round flat cake
garni	with potatoes and vegetables
gâteau	cake
gaufre	wafer; waffle
gelée	jelly
génoise	sponge cake

Gewurztraminer	dry white wine from Alsace
gibelotte de lapin	rabbit stewed in white wine
gibier	game
gigot d'agneau	leg of lamb
gigue de chevreuil	haunch of venison
girolle	chanterelle *(mushroom)*
glace	ice cream
goujon	gudgeon *(fish)*
grand cru	vintage wine
gras-double	tripe
gratin	baked cheese dish with milk and cream
gratin dauphinois	layers of sliced potatoes baked in milk, cream and cheese
gratin de langoustines	scampi *au gratin*
gratin de queues d'écrevisse	crayfish tails *au gratin*
gratinée	baked onion soup
grillé	grilled
grive	thrush
grondin	gurnard (fish)
groseille blanche	white currant
groseille rouge	redcurrant
hachis parmentier	shepherd's pie
hareng mariné	marinated herring
haricots	beans
haricots blancs	haricot beans
haricots de mouton	mutton stew with beans
haricots verts	green beans
homard	lobster
homard à l'américaine	lobster with tomatoes and white wine
hors-d'œuvre	starter
huître	oyster
îles flottantes	floating islands (poached egg whites on top of custard)
infusion	herb tea
jambon	ham
jambon au madère	ham in Madeira wine
jambon de Bayonne	smoked and cured ham
jarret de veau	shin of veal
julienne	soup with chopped vegetables
jus de pomme	apple juice
jus d'orange	orange juice

kir	white wine with blackcurrant liqueur
kirsch	cherry brandy
kugelhof	cake from Alsace
lait	milk
lait grenadine	milk with grenadine cordial
laitue	lettuce
langouste	freshwater crayfish
langoustine	scampi
langue de bœuf	ox tongue
lapereau	young rabbit
lapin	rabbit
lapin à la Lorraine	rabbit in mushroom and cream sauce
lapin à la moutarde	rabbit in mustard sauce
lapin aux pruneaux	rabbit with prunes
lapin de garenne	wild rabbit
lard	bacon
léger	light
légume	vegetable
lentilles	lentils
lièvre	hare
limande	dab, lemon sole
limonade	lemonade
livarot	strong, soft cheese from the north of France
longe	loin
lotte	burbot
loup au fenouil	bass with fennel
macédoine de légumes	mixed vegetables
mache	lamb's lettuce
mangue	mango
maquereau au vin blanc	mackerel in white wine sauce
marc	grape brandy
marcassin	young wild boar
marchand de vin	in red wine sauce
marron	chestnut
massepain	marzipan
menthe	peppermint
menthe à l'eau	mint cordial
menu du jour	today's menu
menu gastronomique	gourmet menu
menu touristique	tourist menu

merlan au vin blanc	whiting in white wine
millefeuille	custard slice
millésime	vintage
morille	morel *(mushroom)*
morue	cod
mouclade	mussels in creamy sauce with saffron, turmeric and white wine
moules à la poulette	mussels in rich white wine sauce
moules marinière	mussels in white wine
mousse au chocolat	chocolate mousse
mousse au jambon	light ham mousse
mousseux	sparkling
moutarde	mustard
mouton	mutton
mulet	mullet
munster	strong cheese
mûre	blackberry
Muscadet	dry white wine from Nantes
myrtille	bilberry
nature	plain
navarin	mutton stew with vegetables
navet	turnip
noisette	hazelnut
noisette d'agneau	small, round lamb steak
noix	walnut
nouilles	noodles
œuf à la coque	boiled egg
œuf dur	hard-boiled egg
œuf en gelée	egg in aspic
œuf mollet	soft-boiled egg
œuf poché	poached egg
œuf sur le plat	fried egg
œufs à la neige	floating islands (poached egg whites on top of custard)
œufs brouillés	scrambled eggs
oie	goose
oignon	onion
omelette au fromage	cheese omelette
omelette au jambon	ham omelette
omelette au naturel	plain omelette
omelette aux champignons	mushroom omelette
omelette aux fines herbes	omelette with herbs

omelette au foie de volaille	omelette with chicken liver
omelette paysanne	omelette with potatoes and bacon
orange givrée	orange sorbet served in an orange
orange pressée	fresh orange juice
oseille	sorrel
oursin	sea urchin
pain	bread
palette de porc	shoulder of pork
palourde	clam
pamplemousse	grapefruit
panade	bread soup
parfait glacé	type of ice cream
pastis	aniseed-flavoured alcoholic drink
pâté de canard	duck pâté
pâté de foie de volaille	chicken liver pâté
pâte feuilletée	puff pastry
pâtes	pasta
paupiettes de veau	slices of veal, rolled up and stuffed
pêche	peach
pêche Melba	peach melba
perdreau	young partridge
perdrix	partridge
petit déjeuner	breakfast
petit pain	roll
petit pois	peas
petit suisse	light, white cream cheese
petite friture	whitebait
petits fours	small fancy pastries
pied de porc	pig's trotter
pigeonneau	young pigeon
pignatelle	small cheese fritter
pilaf de mouton	rice dish with mutton
pintade	guinea fowl
piperade	Basque egg dish with tomatoes and peppers
pissaladière	Provençal dish similar to pizza
pissenlit	dandelion (leaves)
pistache	pistachio
plat du jour	dish of the day
plateau de fromages	cheese board
pochouse	fish casserole with white wine
poire	pear

poire belle Hélène	pear in chocolate sauce
poireau	leek
poisson	fish
poivre	pepper
poivron	red or green pepper
pomme	apple
pomme bonne femme	baked apple
pomme de terre	potato
pommes Dauphine	potato fritters
pommes de terre à l'anglaise	boiled potatoes
pommes de terre en robe de chambre/en robe des champs	jacket potatoes
pommes de terre sautées	fried potatoes
pommes frites	chips, French fries
pommes paille	finely cut chips, French fries
pommes vapeur	steamed potatoes
porc	pork
porto	port
pot-au-feu	beef and vegetable hotpot
potage	soup
potage bilibi	fish and oyster soup
potage Crécy	carrot and rice soup
potage cressonnière	watercress soup
potage Esaü	lentil soup
potage parmentier	leek and potato soup
potage printanier	vegetable soup
potage Saint-Germain	split pea soup
potage velouté	creamy soup
potée	vegetable and meat hotpot
Pouilly-Fuissé	dry white wine from Burgundy
poularde	fattened chicken
poule au pot	chicken and vegetable hotpot
poule au riz	chicken with rice
poulet à l'estragon	chicken in tarragon sauce
poulet basquaise	chicken with *ratatouille*
poulet chasseur	chicken with mushrooms and white wine
poulet créole	chicken in white sauce with rice
poulet rôti	roast chicken
praire	clam
premier cru	vintage wine
provençale	with tomatoes, garlic and herbs

prune	plum
pruneau	prune
pudding	plum pudding
purée	mashed potatoes
purée de marrons	chestnut purée
purée de pommes de terre	mashed potatoes
quatre-quarts	rich cake, similar to Madeira cake
quenelle	meat or fish dumpling
queue de bœuf	oxtail
quiche lorraine	quiche with bacon
râble de chevreuil	saddle of venison
raclette	Swiss dish of melted cheese
radis	radish
ragoût	stew
raie	skate
raie au beurre noir	skate fried in butter
raifort	horseradish
raisin	grape
râpé	grated
rascasse	scorpion fish
ratatouille	dish of stewed peppers, courgettes, aubergines and tomatoes
ravigote	dressing with herbs
reblochon	strong cheese from Savoie
reine-claude	greengage
rémoulade	mayonnaise dressing flavoured with herbs, mustard and capers
rigotte	small goat's cheese from Lyons
rillettes	potted pork or goose meat
ris de veau	veal sweetbread
rissole	meat pie
riz	rice
riz à l'impératrice	sweet rice dish
riz pilaf	spicy rice with meat or seafood
rognon	kidney
rognons au madère	kidneys in Madeira
roquefort	blue cheese
rôti	joint
rôti de porc	roast pork
rouget	mullet
rouille	sauce accompanying *bouillabaisse*

sabayon	zabaglione (whipped egg yolk in Marsala wine)
sablé	shortbread
saint-honoré	cream puff cake
saint-marcellin	goat's cheese
salade	salad, lettuce
salade composée	mixed salad
salade de tomates	tomato salad
salade niçoise	salad of olives, tomatoes, anchovies, tuna, hard-boiled eggs, peppers, lettuce, celery and French beans
salade russe	salad of diced vegetables in mayonnaise
salade verte	green salad
salmis	game stew
salsifis	oyster plant, salsify
sandwich au jambon	ham sandwich
sandwich au saucisson	salami sandwich
sanglier	wild boar
sauce aurore	white sauce with tomato purée
sauce aux câpres	white sauce with capers
sauce béarnaise	thick sauce with eggs and butter
sauce blanche	white sauce
sauce gribiche	dressing with hard-boiled eggs
sauce hollandaise	rich sauce made with eggs, butter and vinegar, served with fish
sauce Madère	Madeira sauce
sauce matelote	wine sauce
sauce Mornay	*béchamel* sauce with cheese
sauce mousseline	*hollandaise* sauce with cream
sauce poulette	sauce made with mushrooms and egg yolks
sauce ravigote	dressing with shallots and herbs
sauce rémoulade	mayonnaise dressing flavoured with herbs, mustard and capers
sauce suprême	creamy sauce
sauce tartare	mayonnaise with herbs and gherkins
sauce veloutée	white sauce with egg yolks and cream
sauce vinot	wine sauce
saucisse	sausage
saucisse de Francfort	frankfurter
saucisse de Strasbourg	beef sausage

saucisson	salami-type sausage
saumon	salmon
saumon fumé	smoked salmon
sauternes	sweet white wine
savarin	crown-shaped rum baba
sec	dry
seiche	cuttlefish
sel	salt
service (non) compris	service (not) included
service 12% inclus	12% service charge included
servir frais	serve cool
sirop	cordial
sole bonne femme	sole in white wine and mushrooms
sole meunière	sole dipped in flour and fried in butter
soufflé au chocolat	chocolate soufflé
soufflé au fromage	cheese soufflé
soufflé au Grand Marnier	soufflé with orange liqueur
soufflé au jambon	ham soufflé
soufflé aux épinards	spinach soufflé
soupe à l'ail	garlic soup
soupe à l'oignon	French onion soup
soupe à l'oseille	sorrel soup
soupe au pistou	thick vegetable soup with basil
soupe aux choux	cabbage soup
soupe aux moules	mussel soup
soupe aux poireaux et pommes de terre	leek and potato soup
soupe aux tomates	tomato soup
soupe de poisson	fish soup
steak au poivre	peppered steak
steak frites	steak and chips
steak haché	minced meat, ground beef
steak tartare	raw minced beef with a raw egg
sucre	sugar
suprême de volaille	chicken in cream sauce
tanche	tench *(fish)*
tarte	tart, pie
tarte aux fraises	strawberry tart
tarte aux pommes	apple tart
tarte frangipane	almond cream tart
tartelette	small tart

arte Tatin	baked apple dish
artine	slice of bread and butter
endrons de veau	breast of veal
errine	pâté
errine du chef	chef's special pâté
ête de veau	calf's head
hé	tea
hé à la menthe	mint tea
hé au lait	tea with milk
hé citron	lemon tea
hon	tuna fish
illeul	lime tea
omate	tomato
omates farcies	stuffed tomatoes
ome de Savoie	white cheese from Savoy
ournedos	round beef steak
ourte	covered pie
ourteau	type of crab
ripes	tripe
ripes à la mode de Caen	tripe in spicy vegetable sauce
ruite au bleu	poached trout
ruite aux amandes	trout fried in butter with almonds
ruite meunière	trout dipped in flour and fried in butter
vacherin	strong, soft cheese from the Jura
vacherin glacé	ice cream meringue
veau	veal
velouté de tomate	cream of tomato soup
vermicelle	vermicelli (very fine pasta used in soups)
verveine	verbena tea
viande	meat
vin	wine
vinaigrette	French dressing
vin blanc	white wine
vin de pays	local wine
vin de table	table wine
vin rosé	rosé wine
vin rouge	red wine
volaille	poultry
VSOP	mature brandy
waterzooi de poulet	chicken with vegetables
yaourt	yogurt

SHOPS AND SERVICES

This chapter covers all sorts of shopping needs and services, an
to start with you'll find some general phrases which can be use
in lots of different places - many of which are named in the li:
below. After the general phrases come some more specific reques
and sentences to use when you've found what you need, be it foo
clothing, repairs, film-developing, a haircut or haggling in th
market. Don't forget to refer to the mini-dictionary for items yo
may be looking for.

Food shops in France are generally open from 8.30 am to 7.3
pm, Tuesday to Saturday. Most hypermarkets are open until 9 c
10 pm. Most baker's are open on Sunday mornings. Other shop
are open from 9 or 10 am to 6.30 or 7 pm. On most Saturday
there's an open-air market in the town square or main street. Her
you can buy food, clothes, china etc at bargain prices. In the cities
shops often don't take a break for lunch and you may see the sig
journée continue (open all day). In small towns and villages
shops will often be closed for two hours at lunch time.

USEFUL WORDS AND PHRASES

antique shop	un magasin d'antiquités	*magazAN dONteekeetay*
audio equipment	radio-hifi	*rahdee-oh ee-fee*
baker's	une boulangerie	*boolONʒree*
bookshop	une librairie	*leebrairee*
boutique	une boutique	*booteek*
butcher's	une boucherie	*booshree*
buy	acheter	*ashtay*
cake shop	une pâtisserie	*patteessree*
camera shop	le photographe	*fohtohgraf*
camping equipment	l'équipement de camping	*aykeepmON duh kONpeeng*
carrier bag	le sac en plastique	*sak ON plasteek*
china	de la porcelaine	*porslen*

80

onfectioner's	la confiserie	*konfeesree*
ost *(verb)*	coûter	*kootay*
raft shop	une boutique d'artisanat	*booteek darteezana*
epartment store	un grand magasin	*grON magazAN*
ry cleaner's	le pressing	*'pressing'*
lectrical goods store	un magasin d'appareils électriques	*magazAN dapparay aylektreek*
shmonger's	une poissonnerie	*pwassonree*
orist's	le fleuriste	*flureest*
ood store	un magasin d'alimentation	*magazAN dall-eemONtass-ion*
ift shop	un magasin de cadeaux	*magazAN duh kaddoh*
rocer's	une épicerie	*aypeessree*
airdresser's	le coiffeur	*kwaffur*
ardware shop	une quincaillerie	*kANkI-ree*
ypermarket	un hypermarché	*eepairmarshay*
ndoor market	un marché couvert	*marshay koovair*
eweller's	une bijouterie	*beeJootree*
adies' wear	des vêtements femmes	*vetmON fam*
aunderette	la laverie automatique	*lavree ohtohmateek*
market	un marché	*marshay*
nenswear	des vêtements hommes	*vetmON omm*
ewsagent's	le tabac-journaux	*tabba Joornoh*
ptician's	l'opticien	*opteess-iAN*
hotography shop	le photographe	*fohtohgraf*
eceipt	un reçu, un ticket de caisse	*ruhsOO, teekay duh kess*
ecord shop	un disquaire	*deeskair*
ale	les soldes	*solld*
hoe repairer's	le cordonnier	*kordonn-yay*
hoe shop	un magasin de chaussure	*magazAN duh shoh-ssOOr*
hop	un magasin	*magazAN*

81

souvenir shop	souvenirs-cadeaux	*soovuhneer kaddo*
sports equipment	l'équipement sportif	*aykeepmON sporte*
sportswear	des articles de sport	*arteek-l duh spor*
stationer's	une papeterie	*pappetree*
supermarket	un supermarché	*sOOpairmarshay*
tailor	le tailleur	*tI-ur*
(for repairs)	la retoucheuse	*ruhtooshuhz*
till	la caisse	*kess*
tobacconist's	le bureau de tabac	*bOOroh duh tabah*
toyshop	un magasin de jouets	*magazAN duh Joo-ay*
travel agent's	une agence de voyages	*aJONss duh vwI-a*
wine merchant's	un marchand de vins	*marshON duh vAN*

Excuse me, where is/are …?
Pardon, pouvez-vous me dire où se trouve … ?
pardON poovay voo muh deer oo suh troov

Where is there a … ? *(shop)*
Où est-ce qu'il y a un/une … ?
oo esskeel-ya AN/OOn

Where is the … department?
Où se trouve le rayon … ?
oo suh troov luh rayON

Where is the main shopping area?
Où se trouve le principal quartier commerçant ?
oo suh troov luh prANseepal katt-yay kommairsON

Is there a market here?
Est-ce qu'il y a un marché ici ?
esskeel-ya AN marshay ee-see

I'd like …
Je voudrais …
Juh voodreh

Do you have …?
Avez-vous … ?
avay voo

How much is this?
Ça coûte combien ?
sa koot kONbyAN

Where do I pay?
Où faut-il payer ?
oo foh-teel pay-ay

Do you take credit cards?
Acceptez-vous les cartes de crédit ?
ak-septay voo lay kart duh kraydee

I think perhaps you've short-changed me
Je crois que vous m'avez rendu trop peu
zhuh krwah kuh voo mavay rONdOO troh puh

Can I have a receipt?
Puis-je avoir un reçu ?
pweezh avwahr AN ruhsOO

Can I have a bag, please ?
Puis-je avoir un sac, s'il vous plaît ?
pweezh avwahr AN sak seel voo pleh

I'm just looking
J'aimerais juste regarder
zhemmereh zhOOst ruhgarday

I'll come back later
Je reviendrai plus tard
zhuh ruhvee-ANdray plOO tar

Do you have any more of these?
En avez-vous d'autres ?
ON avay voo doht-r

83

Have you anything cheaper?
Avez-vous quelque chose de moins cher ?
avay voo kellkuh shohz duh mwAN shair

Have you anything larger/smaller?
Avez-vous quelque chose de plus grand/petit ?
avay voo kellkuh shohz duh plOO grON/puhtee

Can I try it (them) on?
Est-ce que je peux l'essayer (les essayer) ?
esskuh Juh puh lessay-yay (layz essay-yay)

Does it come in other colours?
L'avez-vous dans d'autres coloris ?
lavay voo dON doht-r koloree

Could you gift-wrap it for me?
Pouvez-vous me faire un emballage-cadeau ?
poovay voo muh fair AN ONballaJ kaddoh

I'd like to exchange this. It's faulty
J'aimerais échanger cet article. Il a un défaut
Jemmereh ayshONJay set arteek-l. eel ah AN dayfoh

I'm afraid I don't have the receipt
J'ai bien peur de ne pas avoir le reçu
Jay byAN pur duh nuh paz avwahr luh ruhsOO

Can I have a refund?
Pouvez-vous me rembourser ?
poovay voo muh rONboorsay

My camera isn't working
Mon appareil photo ne marche pas
mON appah-ray fohtoh nuh marsh pa

I want a 36-exposure colour film, 100 ISO
Je voudrais un film couleur de 36 poses, 100 ISO
Juh voodreh AN feelm koolur duh trONt seess poze sON ee-ess-oh

I'd like this film processed
J'aimerais faire développer ce film
Jemmereh fair dayvuhloppay suh feelm

Matt/glossy prints
Epreuves mates/glacées
aypruhv mat/glassay

I'd like one-hour service, please
J'aimerais avoir les épreuves dans une heure, s'il vous plaît
Jemmereh avwahr layz aypruhv dONz OOn ur seel voo pleh

Where can I get this mended? *(shoes/clothes)*
Où est-ce que je peux faire réparer/raccommoder ceci ?
oo esskuh Juh puh fair rayparay/rakomoday suhsee

Can you mend this? *(shoes/clothes)*
Pouvez-vous réparer/raccommoder ceci ?
poovay voo rayparay/rakomoday suhsee

I'd like this skirt/these trousers dry-cleaned
J'aimerais faire nettoyer à sec cette jupe/ce pantalon
Jemmereh fair nettwah-yay ah sek set JOOp/suh pONtalON

When will it/they be ready?
Quand est-ce que ce sera prêt ?
kON esskuh suh suhra preh

I'd like some change for the washing machine/tumble dryer
Je voudrais de la monnaie pour la machine à laver/le séchoir
Juh voodreh duh la monneh poor la masheen ah lavay/luh sayshwahr

How does the machine work?
Comment cette machine fonctionne-t-elle ?
kommON set masheen fONkss-ion tel

I'd like to make an appointment
Je voudrais prendre rendez-vous
Juh voodreh prONdr rONdayvoo

85

I'd like a cut and blow-dry
Je voudrais une coupe et un brushing
juh voodreh OOn koop ay AN brusheeng

With conditioner
Avec démêlant
avek daymelON

No conditioner, thanks
Sans démêlant, merci
sON daymelON mairsee

Just a trim, please
Je voudrais les faire égaliser
juh voodreh lay fair aygaleezay

A bit more off here, please
Un petit peu plus court ici
AN puhtee puh plOO koort ee-see

Not too much off!
N'en coupez pas trop !
nON koopay pa troh

When does the market open?
Quand est-ce que le marché commence ?
kON esskuh luh marshay kommONss

Is there one today in a town nearby?
Est-ce qu'il y en a un aujourd'hui dans une ville avoisinante ?
esskeel yona AN ohjoordwee dONz OOn veel avwahzeenONt

What's the price per kilo?
Combien ça coûte au kilo ?
kONbyAN sa koot oh keeloh

Could you write that down?
Pouvez-vous me l'écrire ?
poovay voo muh laykreer

That's too much! I'll pay ...
C'est beaucoup trop ! Je donne ...
seh bohkoo troh! Juh don

That's fine. I'll take it
C'est bien. Je le prends
seh byAN. Juh luh prON

I'll have a piece of that cheese
Je prendrai un morceau de ce fromage
Juh prONdray AN morsoh duh suh fromaJ

About 250/500 grams
Environ 250/500 grammes
ONveerON duh sON sANkONt/sANk sON gram

A kilo/half a kilo of apples, please
Un kilo/demi-kilo de pommes, s'il vous plaît
AN keeloh/duhmee keeloh duh pom seel voo pleh

A quarter of a kilo of salami, please
Une demi-livre de salami, s'il vous plaît
OOn duhmee leevr duh salamee seel voo pleh

May I taste it?
Puis-je goûter ?
pweeJ gootay

No, I don't like it
Non, je n'aime pas
nON Juh nem pa

That's very nice. I'll take some
C'est très bon. J'en prendrai
seh treh bon. JON prONdray

It isn't what I wanted
Ce n'est pas ce que je voulais
suh neh pa suh kuh Juh vooleh

THINGS YOU'LL SEE

agence de voyages	travel agency
alimentation	grocer's
bon marché	cheap
boucherie	butcher's
boulangerie	bakery
bricolage	DIY supplies
cabines d'essayage	fitting rooms
caddy obligatoire	please take a trolley
caisse	till, cash desk
centre commercial	shopping centre
charcuterie	pork butcher's shop, delicatessen
chocolatier	chocolate shop
coiffeur pour dames/hommes	ladies'/men's hairdresser
confiserie	sweet shop
cordonnier	shoe repairs
droguerie	toiletries and household goods shop
entrée libre	admission free
épicerie	grocer's
épicerie fine	delicatessen
étage inférieur/supérieur	lower/upper floor
fermé le ...	closed on ...
fermeture hebdomadaire le lundi	closed on Mondays
fleuriste	florist
fournitures de bureau	office supplies
fourreur	furrier
frais	fresh
fruits de mer	seafood
glacier	ice cream shop
grand magasin	department store
jouets	toys
journaux	newspapers

→

journée continue	open all day
laverie automatique	launderette
légumes	vegetables
librairie	bookshop
libre-service	self-service
magasin de chaussures	shoe shop
marchand de vin	wine merchant
marché	market
mode	fashion
nous n'acceptons pas les chèques	cheques not accepted
nous ne remboursons pas	we cannot give cash refunds
occasion	bargain, secondhand
ouvert	open
panier obligatoire	please take a basket
papeterie	stationery
parfumerie	perfume and cosmetics shop
pâtisserie	cake shop
payer à l'ordre de ...	payable to ...
photographe	camera shop
poissonerie	fishmonger's
pressing	dry cleaner's
prière de ne pas toucher	please do not touch
primeurs	greengrocer's
prix	price
prix réduit	reduced price
produits d'entretien	household cleaning materials
quincaillerie	hardware shop
rabais	reduction
rayon	department
salon de coiffure	hairdressing salon
soldes	sale
supermarché	supermarket
tabac	tobacconist's
talons minute	shoes heeled while you wait
teinturerie	dry cleaner's

→

89

vêtements enfants	children's wear
vêtements femmes	ladies' wear
vêtements hommes	menswear

THINGS YOU'LL HEAR

Est-ce qu'on s'occupe de vous ?
Are you being served?

Vous désirez ?
Can I help you?

Vous n'avez pas plus petit ?
Haven't you anything smaller? *(money)*

Je suis désolé, mais le stock est épuisé
I'm sorry, we're out of stock

C'est tout ce que nous avons
This is all we have

Et avec ça ?
Will there be anything else?

Combien en voulez-vous ?
How much would you like?

Voulez-vous l'essayer ?
Would you like to try it (on)?

Articles ni repris ni échangés
Goods will not be exchanged

Avez-vous de la monnaie ?
Do you have any change?

SPORT

There is no shortage of sporting facilities in France, whether you want to play tennis, swim, play or watch soccer, rugby, or any other team sport like volley-ball, basket-ball or handball. Between December and April, skiing is very popular, mainly in the Alps which boast a great number of resorts, like those around Grenoble or Chamonix-Mont-Blanc. During the rest of the year the mountains are ideal for hill-walking, climbing and mountain-biking. Windsurfing is also popular, either on the inland lakes, the Mediterranean coast or on the rougher Atlantic Ocean. As for golf, although it has taken off recently in France, it remains an exclusive sport.

There are many sporting holidays available, including cycling, golfing, walking and horse-riding holidays. Information on these can be obtained from a travel agent.

Cycling is more common than in the UK. Bicycles can be hired from over 200 railway stations – you hire a bicycle at one station and return it at another.

USEFUL WORDS AND PHRASES

athletics	l'athlétisme	*attlay-teez-m*
badminton	le badminton	*badmeentON*
ball *(large)*	un ballon	*ballON*
(small)	une balle	*bal*
bicycle	une bicyclette, un vélo	*bee-seeklet, vayloh*
binding *(ski)*	la fixation de ski	*feexass-iON duh skee*
canoe	un canoë	*kano-ay*
canoeing	le canoë-kayac	*kano-ay kI-ak*
cross-country skiing	le ski de fond	*skee duh fON*
go cycling	faire du vélo	*fair dOO vayloh*
diving board	un plongeoir	*plonʒwahr*
downhill skiing	le ski alpin	*skee alpAN*

fish	pêcher	*peshay*
fishing	la pêche	*pesh*
fishing rod	une canne à pêche	*kan ah pesh*
flippers	des palmes	*pal-m*
football	le football, le foot	*footbal, foot*
football match	un match de football	*match duh footbal*
game	une partie	*partee*
goggles	les lunettes	*lOOnet*
golf	le golf	*golf*
golf course	un terrain de golf	*terrAN duh golf*
gymnastics	la gymnastique	*jeemnasteek*
handball	le hand-ball	*ONdbal*
hang-gliding	le deltaplane	*deltaplan*
hunting	la chasse	*shass*
ice rink	une patinoire	*patteenwahr*
lift pass	un forfait pour remonte-pentes	*forfeh poor ruhmONt pONt*
mountain bike	le vélo tout terrain	*vayloh too tairrAN*
mountaineering	l'alpinisme	*alpeeneez-m*
nursery slope	la piste pour débutants	*peest poor daybOOtON*
oxygen bottles	les bouteilles d'oxygène	*bootay doxeejen*
parascending	le parachute ascensionnel	*parashOOt assONss-ionnell*
pedal boat	un pédalo	*paydalloh*
racket	la raquette	*rakket*
ride	faire de l'équitation	*faire duh layk-eetass-iON*
riding	l'équitation	*ayk-eetass-iON*
riding hat	la bombe	*bombe*
rock climbing	la varappe	*varrap*
saddle	la selle	*sell*
sail *(noun)*	la voile	*vwahl*
(verb)	faire de la voile	*fair duh la vwahl*
sailboard	une planche à voile	*plONsh ah vwahl*
sailing	la voile	*vwahl*

skate	faire du patin à glace	*fair dOO pattAN ah glass*
skates	des patins à glace	*pattAN ah glass*
ski *(noun)*	le ski	*skee*
(verb)	faire du ski, skier	*fair dOO skee, skee-ay*
ski boots	des chaussures de ski	*shoh-sOOr duh skee*
skiing	le ski	*skee*
ski lift	le remonte-pente, le télésiège	*ruhmONt pONt, taylaysee-eʒ*
skin diving	la plongée sous-marine	*plONʒay soo mareen*
ski pass	un forfait-skieur	*forfeh skee-ur*
skisticks	les bâtons de ski	*batON duh skee*
ski tow	le téléski	*taylayskee*
ski trail	la piste	*peest*
ski wax	le fart	*far*
sledge	une luge	*looʒ*
snorkel	un tuba	*tOOba*
sports centre	le centre sportif	*sONtr sporteef*
stadium	un stade	*stad*
surfboard	une planche de surf	*plONsh duh sOOrf*
swimming pool	une piscine	*peeseen*
team	une équipe	*aykeep*
tennis	le tennis	*tennees*
tennis court	un court de tennis	*koor duh tennees*
toboggan	le toboggan	*tobogON*
underwater fishing	la pêche sous-marine	*pesh soo mareen*
volleyball	le volleyball, le volley	*vollibal, volli*
water-skiing	le ski nautique	*skee nohteek*
water-skis	des skis nautiques	*skee nohteek*
wet suit	une combinaison de plongée	*kombeenehzON duh plONʒay*
go windsurfing	faire de la planche à voile	*fair duh la plansh ah vwahl*
yacht	un voilier	*vwahlee-ay*

93

Is there an indoor/outdoor pool here?
Est-ce qu'il y a une piscine couverte/en plein air ici ?
esskeel-ya OOn peeseen koovairt/ON plAN air ee-see

Is it safe to swim here?
Est-ce qu'on peut nager ici sans danger ?
esskON puh naʒay ee-see sON dONʒay

Can I fish here?
Est-ce que la pêche est autorisée ici ?
esskuh la pesh et otoreezay ee-see

Is there a golf course near here?
Est-ce qu'il y a un terrain de golf dans les environs ?
esskeel-ya AN terrAN duh golf dON layz ONveerON

Do I have to be a member?
Faut-il être membre ?
foh-teel ettr mONbr

Where can I hire ...?
Où est-ce que je peux louer ... ?
oo esskuh ʒuh puh loo-ay

I would like to hire a bike/some skis
Je voudrais louer une bicyclette/des skis
ʒuh voodreh loo-ay OOn bee-seeklet/day skee

How much does it cost per hour/day?
Quel est le prix pour une heure/journée ?
kell eh luh pree poor OOn ur/ʒoornay

What are the snow conditions like today?
Quelles sont les conditions d'enneigement aujourd'hui ?
kell son lay kondiss-iON dONehʒmON ohʒoordwee

When does the lift start?
Quand est-ce que le remonte-pente commence à fonctionner ?
kONt esskuh luh ruhmONt pONt kommONss ah fONkss-iONay

I would like to take skiing lessons
Je voudrais prendre des leçons de ski
Juh voodreh prONdr day luhssON duh skee

I'd like to try cross-country skiing
Je voudrais essayer le ski de fond
Juh voodreh essay-yay luh skee duh fON

Is it very steep?
Est-ce que la pente est très raide ?
esskuh la pONt eh treh red

Where are the nursery slopes?
Où se trouvent les pistes pour débutants ?
oo suh troov lay peest poor daybOOtON

How much is a daily/weekly lift pass?
Quel est le prix d'un forfait journalier/hebdomadaire pour
 remonte-pentes ?
*kell eh luh pree dAN forfay joornal-yay/ebdoma-dair poor ruhmONt
 pONt*

There's something wrong with this binding
Il y a un problème au niveau de cette fixation
eel-ya AN problaim oh neevoh duh set feexass-iON

I haven't played this before
Je n'ai jamais pratiqué ce sport auparavant
Juh nay Jammeh prateekay suh sporr ohparavON

THINGS YOU'LL SEE

baignade interdite	no swimming
boules	bowling
chasse gardée	hunting preserve
conditions d'enneigement	snow conditions

→

95

conditions pour skier	skiing conditions
courant dangereux	dangerous current
course automobile	racing track
équipements sportifs	sporting facilities
équitation	horse riding
gymnase	gymnasium
leçons de ski nautique	water-skiing lessons
location de bateaux/vélos	boat/bicycle hire
parachute ascensionnel	parascending
patinoire	ice rink
patins à glace	ice skates
pêche interdite	no fishing
pêche sous-marine	underwater fishing
pente	slope
pétanque	French bowling game
piscine	swimming pool
piste balisée	marked ski path
piste cyclable	cycle path
piste de ski	ski track
piste pour débutants	nursery slope
plage	beach
planche à voile	sailboard
plongée interdite	no diving
plongée sous-marine	skin diving
police du port	harbour police
propriété privé interdiction d'entrer	no trespassing
remonte-pente	ski lift; ski tow
risque d'avalanche	danger of avalanche
sentier balisé	marked footpath
stade	stadium
surveillant de plage	lifeguard
télésiège	ski lift
téléski	ski tow
terrain de football	football pitch
vent fort	strong wind

POST OFFICES AND BANKS

Post offices can be identified by the sign **P et T** (**postes et télécommunications**). Opening hours are usually 8 am to 7 pm on weekdays and 8 am to 12 pm on Saturdays. Most post offices close for lunch. Stamps can also be bought in **tabac-journaux** and **bar-tabacs**. Postboxes are yellow.

Most banks are open from 9 am to 5.30 pm and are closed on Saturdays and at lunchtime. There are some variations: some banks open on Saturday morning instead and are closed on Mondays. Foreign currency and traveller's cheques can also be exchanged at some of the larger tourist information centres and hotels, but these usually give less advantageous exchange rates. There are numerous bureaux de change in the main tourist areas in Paris.

The French unit of currency is the **franc** *(frON)*. One **franc** is divided into 100 **centimes** *(sONteem)* and the coins come in 5, 10, 20 and 50 **centimes** and 1, 2, 5 and 10 **francs**. Notes are available in 20, 50, 100, 200 and 500 **francs**.

Credit cards – **les cartes de crédit** – *(kart duh kraydee)* are widely used and accepted for payment in shops, hotels and at petrol stations. It is also possible to withdraw money from a cash dispenser – **un distributeur automatique de billets** – using credit cards, although in most cases there will be a charge for this type of transaction.

USEFUL WORDS AND PHRASES

airmail	par avion	*par av-iON*
bank	la banque	*bONk*
banknote	le billet de banque,	*bee-yay duh bONk,*
	la coupure	*koopOOr*
cash	du liquide	*leekeed*
cash	un distributeur	*deestreebOOtur ohto-*
dispenser	automatique de billets	*mateek duh bee-yay*
change	changer	*shONJay*

97

cheque	un chèque	*shek*
cheque book	un carnet de chèques	*karnay duh shek*
collection	la levée	*luhvay*
counter	le guichet	*geeshay*
credit card	la carte de crédit	*kart duh kraydee*
customs form	un formulaire de douane	*formOOlair duh doo-AN*
delivery	la distribution	*dees-treebOOss-iON*
deposit *(noun)*	un dépôt	*daypoh*
(verb)	déposer	*daypozay*
exchange rate	le taux de change	*toh duh shONJ*
fax *(noun)*	un fax	*fax*
(verb: document)	faxer	*faxay*
fax machine	un fax	*fax*
form	un formulaire	*formOOlair*
international money order	un mandat international	*mONda ANtairnass-iONahl*
letter	une lettre	*lettr*
letter box	la boîte à lettres	*bwat ah lettr*
mail	le courrier	*kooree-ay*
main post office	la poste principale	*posst prANsee-pal*
package	un paquet	*pakkay*
parcel	un colis	*kolee*
post *(noun)*	la poste	*posst*
(verb)	poster	*posstay*
postage rates	les tarifs postaux	*tareef postoh*
postal order	un mandat postal	*mONda postal*
post box	la boîte postale	*bwat postal*
postcard	une carte postale	*kart postal*
postcode	le code postal	*kod postal*
poste-restante	la poste restante	*posst restONt*
postman	le facteur	*faktur*
post office	la poste	*posst*
pound sterling	la livre sterling	*leevr stairleen*
registered letter	une lettre recommandée	*lettr ruh-kommONday*
stamp	un timbre	*tANbr*

98

surface mail	par voie de terre	*par vwah duh tair*
telegram	un télégramme	*taylaygram*
traveller's cheque	le chèque de voyage	*shek duh vwI-yaʃ*
withdraw	retirer	*ruhteeray*
withdrawal	un retrait	*ruhtreh*

How much is a letter/postcard to England?
Quel est le tarif pour une lettre/carte postale pour l'Angleterre ?
kell eh luh tareef poor OOn lettr/kart postal poor lONgl-tair

I would like three 2 francs 50 stamps
Je voudrais trois timbres à deux francs cinquante
ʃuh voodreh trwah tANbr ah duh frON sANkONt

I want to register this letter
Je voudrais envoyer cette lettre en recommandé
ʃuh voodreh ONvwah-yay set lettr ON ruh-kommONday

I want to send this parcel to Scotland
Je voudrais envoyer ce colis en Ecosse
ʃuh voodreh ONvwah-yay suh kolee ON aykoss

How long does the post to America take?
Combien de temps mettent les lettres pour les Etats-Unis ?
kONbyAN duh tON met lay lettr poor lays aytasOOnee

Where can I post this?
Où est-ce que je peux poster ceci ?
oo esskuh ʃuh puh postay suhsee

Is there any mail for me?
Est-ce qu'il y a du courrier pour moi ?
esskeel-ya dOO kooree-ay poor mwah

I'd like to send a telegram/fax
Je voudrais envoyer un télégramme/un fax
ʃuh voodreh ONvwah-yay AN taylaygram/AN fax

This is to go airmail
Cela doit être expédié par avion
suhla dwaht ettr expaydie-ay par av-iON

I'd like to change this into French francs
J'aimerais changer ceci en francs français
Jemmereh shONJay suhsee ON frON frONsay

I'd like that in 100 franc notes
Je voudrais cela en coupures de 100 francs
Juh voodreh suhla ON koopOOr duh sON frON

Can I cash these traveller's cheques?
Est-ce que je peux encaisser ces chèques de voyage ?
esskuh Juh puh ONkehssay say shek duh vwI-yaJ

What is the exchange rate for the pound?
Quel est le taux de change de la livre ?
kell eh luh toh duh shONJ duh la leevr

Can I draw cash using this credit card?
Est-ce que je peux retirer de l'argent avec cette carte de crédit ?
esskuh Juh puh ruhteeray duh larJON avek set kart duh kraydee

Could you give me smaller notes?
Pourriez-vous me donner des coupures plus petites ?
pooree-ay voo muh donnay day koopOOr plOO puhteet

THINGS YOU'LL SEE

accusé de réception	acknowledgement of receipt
affranchissement	postage
à l'étranger	abroad
autres destinations	other destinations
banque	bank
boîte à lettres	letter box
bureau de poste	post office

➞

bureau le plus proche ...	nearest post office ...
caissier	cashier
carnet de timbres	book of stamps
change	exchange
change de devises	currency exchange
colis	parcel
courrier recommandé	registered mail
destinataire	addressee
devises étrangères	foreign currency
distributeur automatique de billets	cash dispenser
expéditeur	sender
frais	charges
guichet	counter
heures des levées	collection times
heures d'ouverture	opening hours
imprimé	printed matter
localité	place
mandat postal	postal order
ne pas affranchir	freepost
paquet	package
par avion	airmail
point argent	cash point
postes	mail
prochaine levée	next collection
P et T (postes et télécommunications)	post office (with telephone)
renseignements	enquiries
tarifs postaux	postage rates
tarifs postaux intérieurs	inland postage
tarifs postaux pour l'étranger	overseas postage
taux de change	rate of exchange
timbre	stamp
transactions avec l'étranger	overseas business
ville	town

TELEPHONES

Telephone boxes in France are square stainless steel kiosks. They nearly all take phonecards and there are very few coin-operated phones. Phonecards can be bought at post offices, **tabac-journaux** and **bar-tabacs**.

To telephone the UK from France, dial 19 and wait for the musical signal, then dial 44 followed by the area code and the number you want. (Note, do **not** dial the 0 which prefixes all area code numbers in the UK.) The dialling tone and engaged tone are the same as in the UK. The ringing tone is a repeated long tone and when a number is unobtainable a voice says: '**Il n'y a pas d'abonné au numéro que vous avez demandé, veuillez consulter l'annuaire ou l'opérateur**'.

All French telephone numbers have eight digits and are read out in pairs of numbers, ie 45 82 64 32 is said '**quarante-cinq, quatre-vingt-deux, soixante-quatre, trente-deux**' (forty-five, eighty-two, sixty-four, thirty-two). When dialling from Paris to somewhere outside Paris, dial 16 then the eight digit number. When dialling to Paris from outside, the eight digit number should be preceded by 16 1.

For directory enquiries, dial 12 and for the operator 13.

USEFUL WORDS AND PHRASES

call *(noun)*	un communication	*kommOOneekass-iON*
(verb)	appeler	*applay*
cardphone	le téléphone à carte	*taylayfon ah kart*
code	l'indicatif	*ANdeekateef*
crossed line	une ligne embrouillée	*leen-yuh ONbrwee-ay*
dial	composer un numéro	*kompozay AN nOOmayroh*
dialling tone	la tonalité	*tonaleetay*
emergency	l'urgence	*OOrJONss*
enquiries	les renseignements	*rONsen-yuhmON*
extension	le poste, l'extension	*posst, extONss-iON*
international	international	*ANtairnass-ionahl*

number	le numéro	nOOmayroh
operator	l'opérateur	opayratur
(female)	l'opératrice	opay-ratreess
phonecard	la télécarte	taylaykart
phone directory	l'annuaire, le bottin	annOO-air, bottAN
receiver	le combiné	kONbeenay
reverse charge	une communication	kommOOneekass-iON
call	en P.C.V.	ON pay say vay
telephone	le téléphone	taylayfon
telephone box	une cabine	kabeen
wrong number	un faux numéro	foh nOOmayroh

Where is the nearest phone box?
Où se trouve la cabine téléphonique la plus proche ?
oo suh troov la kabeen taylay-foneek la plOO prosh

Is there a telephone directory?
Est-ce qu'il y a un annuaire ?
esskeel-ya AN annOO-air

I would like to reverse the charges
Je voudrais téléphoner en P.C.V.
Juh voodreh taylayfonay ON pay say vay

I would like a number in Asnières
Je voudrais un numéro à Asnières
Juh voodreh AN nOOmayroh ah assnee-air

Can you give me an outside line?
Pouvez-vous me donner une ligne extérieure ?
poovay voo muh donnay OOn leen-yuh extayree-ur

How do I get an outside line?
Comment est-ce que je peux obtenir une ligne extérieure ?
kommON esskuh Juh puh obtuhneer OOn leen-yuh extayree-ur

Hello, this is Anne speaking
Allô ! Anne à l'appareil
allo ! Anne ah lapparay

103

Is that Jean?
C'est Jean ?
seh JON

Speaking *(said by a man/woman)*
Lui-même/elle-même
lwee mem/el mem

I would like to speak to Nadine
Je voudrais parler à Nadine
Juh voodreh parlay ah nadeen

Extension 423, please
Le poste 423, s'il vous plaît
luh posst kattr sON vAN trwah seel voo pleh

Please tell him/her David called
Pouvez-vous lui dire que David a téléphoné ?
poovay voo lwee deer kuh David ah taylayfonay

Ask him/her to call me back please
Pouvez-vous lui demander de me rappeler ?
poovay voo lwee duhmONday duh muh rapplay

My number is 45 82 64 32
Mon numéro est le quarante-cinq, quatre-vingt-deux, soixante-
quatre, trente-deux
*mON nOOmayroh eh luh karONt sANk, kattr vAN duh, swassONt
kattr, trONt duh*

Do you know where he/she is?
Savez-vous où je peux le/la contacter ?
savay voo oo Juh puh luh/la kontaktay

When will he/she be back?
Savez-vous quand il/elle sera de retour ?
savay voo kONt eel/el suhra duh ruhtoor

Could you leave him/her a message?
Pouvez-vous lui laisser un message ?
poovay voo lwee lessay AN muhssaJ

'll ring back later
e rappellerai plus tard
uh rappelray plOO tar

Sorry, I've got the wrong number
Excusez-moi, je me suis trompé de numéro
xkOOzay mwah Juh muh swee trONpay duh nOOmayroh

Sorry, you've got the wrong number
e regrette, vous avez un faux numéro
uh ruhgret vooz avay AN foh nOOmayroh

THE ALPHABET

a	*ah*	**h**	*ash*	**o**	*o*	**v**	*vay*
b	*bay*	**i**	*ee*	**p**	*pay*	**w**	*doobluhvay*
c	*say*	**j**	*jee*	**q**	*kOO*	**x**	*eeks*
d	*day*	**k**	*ka*	**r**	*air*	**y**	*ee-grek*
e	*ay*	**l**	*el*	**s**	*ess*	**z**	*zed*
f	*ef*	**m**	*em*	**t**	*tay*		
g	*jay*	**n**	*en*	**u**	*OO*		

THINGS YOU'LL SEE

annuaire	telephone directory
bottin	telephone directory
cabine téléphonique	telephone box
communication interurbaine	long-distance call
communication urbaine	local call
composez	dial
crédit ... unités	... units remaining/in credit
décrochez	lift the receiver
en dérangement	out of order
fermez le volet svp	close the flap
frais	charges

→

105

indicatif	code
introduire carte ou composer numéro libre	insert card or dial freephone
numéro direct	direct dialling
numéro vert	freephone
pièce	coin
raccrochez svp	replace the receiver
réclamations	faults service
renseignements	directory enquiries
renseignements internationaux	international directory enquiries
retirez votre carte	remove your card
télécarte	phonecard
téléphone à carte	cardphone
unité	unit
veuillez patienter	please wait

REPLIES YOU MAY BE GIVEN

A quel numéro pouvons-nous vous joindre ?
At what number can we contact you?

A qui désirez-vous parler ?
Who would you like to speak to?

Vous avez un faux numéro
You've got the wrong number

Qui est à l'appareil ?
Who's speaking?

C'est de la part de qui ?
Who shall I say is calling?

→

Lui-même/elle-même
Speaking

J'écoute
Speaking

La ligne est encombrée
The line is busy

Ne quittez pas
Hold the line

Ne raccrochez pas
Hold the line

Pourriez-vous rappeler plus tard ?
Could you phone back later?

Quel numéro demandez-vous ?
Which number do you want?

Quel est votre numéro ?
What is your number?

Désolé, il/elle n'est pas là
Sorry, he/she is not in

Il/elle sera de retour à six heures
He/she will be back at 6 pm

Pouvez-vous rappeler demain ?
Please call again tomorrow

Le numéro que vous avez demandé n'est pas en service actuellement. Nous regrettons de ne pouvoir donner suite à votre appel
The number you have dialled is not in use. We're sorry we cannot put your call through

EMERGENCIES

Information on local health services can be obtained from tourist information offices, but in an emergency dial 18 for an ambulance or the fire brigade. Dial 17 for the police. In the event of your car breaking down, there are phones at intervals along motorways and main roads.

USEFUL WORDS AND PHRASES

accident	un accident	*ak-seedON*
ambulance	une ambulance	*ONbOOlONss*
assault	attaquer	*attakay*
breakdown	une panne	*pan*
break down	tomber en panne	*tONbay ON pan*
breakdown recovery	le dépannage	*daypannaʒ*
burglar	un cambrioleur	*kONbri-olur*
burglary	un cambriolage	*kONbri-olaʒ*
casualty department	le service des urgences	*sairveess dayz OOrʒONss*
crash	un accident	*ak-seedON*
emergency	l'urgence	*OOrʒONss*
fire	le feu	*fuh*
fire brigade	les pompiers	*pONp-yay*
flood	une inondation	*eenONdass-iON*
injured	blessé	*blessay*
lose	perdre	*pairdr*
pickpocket	le pickpocket	*'pickpocket'*
police	la police	*poleess*
police station	le poste de police	*posst duh poleess*
steal	voler	*volay*
theft	un vol	*vol*
thief	le voleur	*volur*
tow	remorquer	*ruhmorkay*

Help!
À l'aide !
ah led

Look out!
Attention !
attONss-iON

Stop!
Arrêtez !
arretay

This is an emergency!
C'est une urgence !
set OOn OOrJONss

Get an ambulance!
Appelez une ambulance !
applay OOn ONbOOlONss

Hurry up!
Faites vite !
fet veet

Please send an ambulance to ...
Veuillez envoyer une ambulance à ...
vuh-yay ONvwah-yay OOn ONbOOlONss ah

Please come to ...
Veuillez venir à ...
vuh-yay vuhneer ah

My address is ...
Mon adresse est ...
mON adress eh

We've had a break-in
Nous avons été cambriolés
nooz avON aytay kONbri-olay

109

There's a fire at ...
Il y a le feu à ...
eelya luh fuh ah

Someone's been injured/knocked down
Quelqu'un a été blessé/renversé
kellkAN ah aytay blessay/rONvairsay

He's passed out
Il a perdu connaissance
eel ah pairdOO konnessONss

My passport/car has been stolen
On a volé mon passeport/ma voiture
ON ah volay mON passpor/ma vwahtOOr

I've lost my traveller's cheques
J'ai perdu mes chèques de voyage
jay pairdOO may shek duh vwI-aj

I want to report a stolen credit card
Je veux signaler le vol d'une carte de crédit
juh vuh seen-yallay luh vol dOOn kart duh kraydee

It was stolen from my room
On l'a volée dans ma chambre
ON la volay dON ma shONbr

I lost it in the park/on the train
Je l'ai perdue dans le parc/dans le train
juh lay pairdOO dON luh park/dON luh trAN

My luggage has gone missing
On a égaré mes bagages
ON ah aygaray may bagaj

Has my luggage turned up yet?
A-t-on retrouvé mes bagages ?
attON ruhtroovay may bagaj

The registration number is ...
La plaque d'immatriculation est ...
la plak deematreekOOlass-iON eh

I've had a crash
J'ai eu un accident
Jay OO AN ak-seedON

My car's been broken into
On a fracturé ma voiture
ON ah fraktOOray ma vwahtOOr

I've been mugged
On m'a agressé
ON ma agressay

My son's missing
Mon fils a disparu
mON feess ah deesparOO

He has fair/brown hair
Il a les cheveux blonds/bruns
eel ah lay shuhvuh blON/brAN

He's ... years old
Il a ... ans
eel ah ... ON

I've locked myself out
Je me suis enfermé dehors
Juh muh sweez ONfairmay duh-or

He's drowning
Il se noie
eel suh nwah

She can't swim
Elle ne sait pas nager
el nuh seh pa naJay

THINGS YOU'LL SEE

feu	fire
formez le ...	dial ...
hôpital	hospital
pharmacie de garde	late-night chemist
police de la route	traffic police
poste de police	police station
premiers secours	first aid
secours de montagne	mountain rescue
service des urgences	casualty department
service non-stop	24-hour service
surveillant	lifeguard
urgences	emergencies

THINGS YOU'LL HEAR

Quelle est votre adresse ?
What's your address?

Où êtes-vous ?
Where are you?

Pouvez-vous le/la décrire ?
Can you describe it/him/her?

Quel âge a-t-il/elle ?
How old is he/she?

Quand est-ce arrivé ?
When did it happen?

HEALTH

Under EC Social Security regulations visitors from the UK qualify for free medical treatment on the same basis as the French themselves. If you want to make sure of being in possession of all necessary documentation, you should obtain a T4 from a main post office, fill in the attached E111 and get it stamped at the post office before travelling. With the E111, you'll also get a leaflet explaining how to obtain treatment.

A chemist's is called a **pharmacie**. At night and on Sundays there is **la pharmacie de garde** (duty chemist). You can find its address in the local newspaper, in the window of any chemist or through the local **commissariat de police**. If you have a prescription from your doctor at home, it will have to be rewritten by a French doctor. Some chemists specialize in English medicine and if you have not brought (or if they don't stock) the remedy you require, they can always recommend a substitute.

USEFUL WORDS AND PHRASES

accident	un accident	*ak-seedON*
ambulance	une ambulance	*ONbOOlONss*
anaemic	anémique	*annaymeek*
appendicitis	une appendicite	*appONdee-seet*
appendix	l'appendice	*appONdeess*
aspirin	de l'aspirine	*aspeereen*
asthma	l'asthme	*ass-m*
backache	le mal de dos	*mal duh doh*
bandage	un pansement	*pONssmON*
bite *(by dog)*	une morsure	*morsOOr*
(by insect)	une piqûre	*peekOOr*
bladder	la vessie	*vessee*
blister	une ampoule	*ONpool*
blood	du sang	*sON*
blood donor	un donneur de sang	*donnur duh sON*
burn	une brûlure	*brOOlOOr*
cancer	le cancer	*kONsair*

113

chemist	la pharmacie	*farmassee*
chest	la poitrine	*pwattreen*
chickenpox	la varicelle	*varree-sel*
cold	un rhume	*rOOm*
concussion	une commotion cérébrale	*kommoss-iON sayraybral*
constipation	la constipation	*kONstee-pass-iON*
contact lenses	des lentilles de contact	*lONtee duh kONtakt*
corn	un cor	*kor*
cough	la toux	*too*
cut	une coupure	*koopOOr*
dentist	le dentiste	*dONteest*
diabetes	le diabète	*dee-abet*
diarrhoea	la diarrhée	*dee-array*
dizzy	le vertige	*vairteeƷ*
doctor *(male)*	le docteur	*doktur*
(female)	la doctoresse	*doktoress*
earache	le mal d'oreille	*mal doray*
fever	la fièvre	*fee-evr*
filling	un plombage	*plONbaƷ*
first aid	premiers soins	*pruhm-yay swAN*
flu	la grippe	*greep*
fracture	une fracture	*fraktOOr*
German measles	la rubéole	*rOObay-ol*
glasses	des lunettes	*lOO-net*
haemorrhage	une hémorragie	*aymorraƷee*
hayfever	le rhume des foins	*rOOm day fwAN*
headache	le mal de tête	*mal duh tet*
heart	le cœur	*kur*
heart attack	une crise cardiaque	*kreez kardee-ak*
hospital	l'hôpital	*opeetahl*
ill	malade	*malad*
indigestion	une indigestion	*ANdeeƷest-iON*
injection	une piqûre	*peekOOr*
itch	des démangeaisons	*daymONƷezON*
kidney	le rein	*rAN*

lump	une grosseur	*grossur*
measles	la rougeole	*rooJol*
migraine	la migraine	*meegren*
mumps	les oreillons	*oray-yON*
nausea	la nausée	*nozay*
nurse	l'infirmier	*ANfeerm-yay*
(female)	l'infirmière	*ANfeermee-air*
operation	une opération	*opayrass-iON*
optician	un opticien	*optees-yAN*
pain	une douleur	*doolur*
penicillin	la pénicilline	*paynee-seeleen*
plaster *(sticky)*	le sparadrap	*sparadra*
plaster of Paris	le plâtre	*platr*
pneumonia	une pneumonie	*p-nuhmonee*
pregnant	enceinte	*ONsANt*
prescription	une ordonnance	*ordonnONss*
rheumatism	des rhumatismes	*rOOmattees-m*
scald	une brûlure	*brOOlOOr*
scratch	une égratignure	*aygratteen-yOOr*
smallpox	la variole	*varree-ol*
sore throat	le mal de gorge	*mal duh gorJ*
splinter	une écharde	*ayshard*
sprain	une entorse	*ONtorss*
sting	une piqûre	*peekOOr*
stomach	l'estomac	*estoma*
temperature	la température	*tONpayratOOr*
tonsils	les amygdales	*ammeedal*
toothache	le mal de dents	*mal duh dON*
travel sickness	le mal des transports	*mal day trONspor*
ulcer	un ulcère	*OOl-sair*
vaccination	un vaccin	*vakksAN*
vomit	vomir	*vomeer*
whooping cough	la coqueluche	*koklOOsh*

I have a pain in …
J'ai mal au/à la …
Jay mal oh/ah la

I do not feel well
Je ne me sens pas bien
Juh nuh muh sON pa byAN

I feel faint
Je vais m'évanouir
Juh veh mayvanweer

I feel sick
J'ai envie de vomir
Jay ONvee duh vomeer

I feel dizzy
J'ai la tête qui tourne
Jay la tet kee toorn

It hurts here
J'ai mal ici
Jay mal ee-see

It's a sharp/dull pain
C'est une douleur aiguë/sourde
set OOn doolur ay-gOO/soord

It hurts all the time
La douleur est constante
la doolur eh kONstONt

It only hurts now and then
C'est douloureux de temps en temps
seh doolooruh duh tON zON tON

It hurts when you touch it
C'est douloureux au toucher
seh doolooruh oh tooshay

It hurts more at night
C'est douloureux surtout la nuit
seh doolooruh sOOrtoo la nwee

It stings/aches
Ça pique/fait mal
sa peek/feh mal

I have a temperature
J'ai de la fièvre
jay duh la fee-evr

I need a prescription for …
J'ai besoin d'une ordonnance pour …
jay buhzwAN dOOn ordonnONss poor

I normally take …
Je prends habituellement …
juh prON abeetOO-elmON

I'm allergic to …
Je suis allergique à …
juh sweez allerjeek ah

Have you got anything for …?
Avez-vous quelque chose contre …?
avay voo kellkuh shohz kONtr

Do I need a prescription for …?
Me faut-il une ordonnance pour …?
muh foh-teel OOn ordonnONss poor

I have lost a filling
J'ai perdu un plombage
jay pairdOO AN plONbaj

Will he/she be all right?
Va-t-il/elle se remettre ?
vateel/el suh ruhmettr

Will he/she need an operation?
Est-ce qu'il/elle devra subir une opération ?
essk eel/el duhvra sOObeer OOn opayrass-iON

117

How is he/she?
Comment va-t-il/elle ?
kommON vateel/el

THINGS YOU'LL SEE

anesthésie générale	general anaesthetic
anesthésie locale	local anaesthetic
cabinet dentaire	dentist's surgery
cabinet médical	doctor's surgery
dermatologue	dermatologist
généraliste	GP
gynécologue	gynaecologist
hôpital	hospital
infirmerie	infirmary
médecin	doctor
oculiste	eye specialist
ophtalmologue	ophthalmologist
oto-rhino-laryngologiste	ear, nose and throat specialist
pédiatre	paediatrician
pharmacie	chemist's
pharmacie de garde	duty chemist
pharmacie de service	duty chemist
premiers soins	first aid
salle d'attente	waiting room
service	ward
service d'urgence	emergency ward
S.O.S Médecin	24-hour emergency medical service found in large towns

REPLIES YOU MAY BE GIVEN

Prendre ... comprimés à la fois
Take ... pills/tablets at a time

Prendre ... comprimés ... fois par jour
Take ... pills/tablets ... times a day

Avec de l'eau
With water

Mâchez-les
Chew them

A prendre au coucher
To be taken at bedtime

Le matin à jeun
First thing in the morning on an empty stomach

Une/deux/trois fois par jour
Once/twice/three times a day

Au coucher seulement
Only when you go to bed

Que prenez-vous habituellement?
What do you normally take?

Je pense que vous devriez voir un docteur
I think you should see a doctor

Je regrette, nous n'avons pas cela
I'm sorry, we don't have that

Il vous faut une ordonnance pour ça
For that you need a prescription

On ne trouve pas cela ici
You cannot get that here

CONVERSION TABLES

DISTANCES

A mile is 1.6km. To convert kilometres to miles, divide the km by 8 and multiply by 5. Convert miles to km by dividing the miles by 5 and multiplying by 8.

miles	0.62	1.24	1.86	2.43	3.11	3.73	4.35	6.21
miles or km	**1**	**2**	**3**	**4**	**5**	**6**	**7**	**10**
km	1.61	3.22	4.83	6.44	8.05	9.66	11.27	16.10

WEIGHTS

The kilogram is equivalent to 2lb 3oz. To convert kg to lbs, divide by 5 and multiply by 11. One ounce is about 28 grams, and eight ounces about 227 grams; 1lb is therefore about 454 grams.

lbs	2.20	4.41	6.61	8.82	11.02	13.23	19.84	22.04
lbs or kg	**1**	**2**	**3**	**4**	**5**	**6**	**9**	**10**
kg	0.45	0.91	1.36	1.81	2.27	2.72	4.08	4.53

TEMPERATURE

To convert Celsius degrees into Fahrenheit, the accurate method is to multiply the °C figure by 1.8 and add 32. Similarly, to convert °F to °C, subtract 32 from the °F figure and divide by 1.8.

°C	-10	0	5	10	20	30	36.9	40	100
°F	14	32	41	50	68	77	98.4	104	212

LIQUIDS

A litre is about 1.75 pints; a gallon is roughly 4.5 litres.

gals	0.22	0.44	1.10	2.20	4.40	6.60	11.00
gals or litres	**1**	**2**	**5**	**10**	**20**	**30**	**50**
litres	4.54	9.10	22.73	45.46	90.92	136.40	227.30

TYRE PRESSURES

lb/sq in	18	20	22	24	26	28	30	33
kg/sq cm	1.3	1.4	1.5	1.7	1.8	2.0	2.1	2.3

MINI-DICTIONARY

The feminine of most adjectives is formed by adding 'e' to the masculine form given in this dictionary and consequently pronouncing the final consonant (eg, petit *puhtee*, petite *puhteet*). Irregular feminine forms are indicated after the abbreviation *(fem)*.

a un/une *(see p 5)*
about: about 16 environ seize
accelerator l'accélérateur
accident l'accident
accommodation l'hébergement
ache la douleur
adaptor *(plug)* la prise multiple
  (voltage) l'adaptateur
address l'adresse
adhesive l'adhésif
aftershave l'après-rasage
again de nouveau
against contre
agent l'agent
Aids SIDA
air l'air
air-conditioning la climatisation
aircraft l'avion
air hostess l'hôtesse de l'air
airline la compagnie aérienne
airport l'aéroport
airport bus la navette (pour
  l'aéroport)
alarm clock le réveil
alcohol l'alcool
Algeria l'Algérie
Algerian algérien
  (man) un Algérien
  (woman) une Algérienne
all tout
  all the streets toutes les rues
  that's all c'est tout
almost presque
alone seul

Alps les Alpes
already déjà
always toujours
am: I am je suis
ambulance l'ambulance
America l'Amérique
American américain
  (man) un Américain
  (woman) une Américaine
and et
Andorra Andorre
ankle la cheville
anorak l'anorak
another *(different)* un/une autre
  another coffee, please encore
  un café, s'il vous plaît
anti-freeze l'antigel
antique shop le magasin
  d'antiquités
antiseptic l'antiseptique
apartment l'appartement
aperitif l'apéritif
appetite l'appétit
apple la pomme
application form le formulaire de
  demande
appointment le rendez-vous
apricot l'abricot
are: you are vous êtes
  (singular, familiar) tu es
  we are nous sommes
  they are ils/elles sont
arm le bras
arrival l'arrivée

121

arrive arriver
art l'art
art gallery le musée d'art
artist l'artiste
as: as soon as possible dès que
  possible
ashtray le cendrier
asleep endormi
  he's asleep il dort
aspirin l'aspirine
at: at the post office à la poste
  at the café au café
  at 3 o'clock à 3 heures
attractive attirant
aunt la tante
Australia l'Australie
Australian australien
  (man) un Australien
  (woman) une Australienne
automatic automatique
away: is it far away? est-ce que
  c'est loin ?
  go away! allez-vous en !
awful affreux
axe la hache
axle l'essieu

baby le bébé
back *(not front)* l'arrière
  (body) le dos
 I'll come back tomorrow je
  reviendrai demain
bacon le bacon
  bacon and eggs des œufs au
  bacon
bad mauvais
baggage claim la réclamation de
  bagages
bait l'appât
bake cuire
baker's la boulangerie
balcony le balcon
ball *(football etc)* le ballon
  (tennis etc) la balle

ballpoint pen le stylo-bille
banana la banane
band *(musicians)* le groupe
bandage le pansement
bank la banque
banknote le billet
bar le bar
  bar of chocolate une tablette de
  chocolat
barbecue le barbecue
barber's le coiffeur
bargain une affaire
basement le sous-sol
basin *(sink)* le lavabo
basket le panier
bath le bain
  (tub) la baignoire
  to have a bath prendre un bain
bathroom la salle de bain
battery *(car)* la batterie
  (torch) la pile
beach la plage
beans les haricots
beard la barbe
beautiful beau, *(fem)* belle
because parce que
bed le lit
bed linen les draps
bedroom la chambre
beef le bœuf
beer la bière
before avant
beginner le débutant
  (female) la débutante
behind derrière
beige beige
Belgian belge
  (man) un Belge
  (woman) une Belge
Belgium la Belgique
bell *(church)* la cloche
  (door) la sonnette
below ... sous ...
belt la ceinture

beside à côté de
best: the best le meilleur
better mieux
between ... entre ...
bicycle la bicyclette, le vélo
big grand
bill l'addition
bin liner le sac poubelle
bird l'oiseau
birthday l'anniversaire
 happy birthday! joyeux
 anniversaire !
biscuit le biscuit
bite *(noun: by dog)* la morsure
 (by snake, insect) la piqûre
 (verb: dog) mordre
 (insect, snake) piquer
bitter amer
black noir
blackberry la mûre
blackcurrant le cassis·
blanket la couverture
bleach *(noun)* l'eau de Javel ®
 (verb) décolorer
blind *(cannot see)* aveugle
 (window) le store
blister l'ampoule
blizzard la tempête de neige
blond *(adj)* blond
blood le sang
blouse le chemisier
blue bleu
boat le bateau
 (smaller) la barque
body le corps
boil *(verb)* bouillir
boiler le chauffe-eau
bolt *(noun: on door)* le verrou
 (verb) verrouiller
bone l'os
 (fish) l'arête
bonnet *(car)* le capot
book *(noun)* le livre
 (verb) réserver

bookshop la librairie
boot *(car)* le coffre
 (footwear) la botte
border la frontière
boring ennuyeux
born: I was born in ... je suis né
 en ...
both les deux
 both of them tous les deux
 both of us nous deux
 both ... and ... ... et ... à la fois
bottle la bouteille
bottle-opener le décapsuleur,
 l'ouvre-bouteille
bottom le fond
 (part of body) le derrière
bowl le bol
box la boîte
box office *(theatre etc)* le bureau de
 location
boy le garçon
boyfriend le petit ami
bra le soutien-gorge
bracelet le bracelet
braces les bretelles
brake *(noun)* le frein
 (verb) freiner
brandy le cognac
bread le pain
breakdown *(car)* la panne
 (nervous) la dépression
 I've had a breakdown *(car)* je
 suis tombé en panne
breakfast le petit déjeuner
breathe respirer
bridge le pont
briefcase l'attaché-case
British britannique
Brittany la Bretagne
brochure la brochure
broken cassé
 broken leg la jambe cassée
brooch la broche
brother le frère

brown marron
bruise le bleu
brush *(noun)* la brosse
  (paint) le pinceau
  (broom) le balai
  (verb) brosser
Brussels Bruxelles
bucket le seau
building le bâtiment
bumper le pare-chocs
burn *(noun)* la brûlure
  (verb) brûler
bus le bus
business les affaires
  it's none of your business cela
  ne vous regarde pas
busker le musicien des rues
bus station la gare routière
busy *(occupied)* occupé
  (street) animé
but mais
butcher's la boucherie
butter le beurre
button le bouton
buy acheter
by: by the window près de la
  fenêtre
  by Friday d'ici vendredi
  by myself tout seul
  written by ... écrit par ...

cabbage le chou
cable car le téléphérique
café le café
cagoule le K-way ®
cake le gâteau
cake shop la pâtisserie
calculator la calculette
call: what's it called? comment
  est-ce que ça s'appelle ?
camcorder le caméscope
camera l'appareil-photo
campsite le terrain de camping
camshaft l'arbre à cames

can *(tin)* la boîte de conserve
can *(able)* pouvoir
  can I have ...? puis-je avoir ... ?
  can you ...? pouvez-vous ... ?
Canada le Canada
Canadian canadien
  (man) un Canadien
  (woman) une Canadienne
canal le canal
candle la bougie
canoe le canoë
cap *(hat)* la casquette
  (bottle) la capsule
car la voiture
caravan la caravane
carburettor le carburateur
card la carte
cardigan le gilet
careful prudent
  careful! attention !
  be careful! soyez prudent !
caretaker le/la concierge
carpet le tapis
carriage *(train)* la voiture, le wagon
carrot la carotte
carry-cot le porte-bébé
case la valise
cash l'argent
  to pay cash payer en liquide
cash dispenser le distributeur
  automatique de billets
cassette la cassette
cassette player le lecteur de
  cassettes
castle le château
cat le chat
cathedral la cathédrale
cauliflower le chou-fleur
cave la grotte
cemetery le cimetière
central heating le chauffage
  central
centre le centre
certificate le certificat

chair la chaise
change *(noun: money)* la monnaie
  (verb: money) changer
  (clothes) se changer
Channel la Manche
Channel Islands les îles Anglo-Normandes
Channel Tunnel le tunnel sous la Manche
cheap bon marché, pas cher
check-in l'enregistrement des bagages
check in faire enregistrer ses bagages
cheers! *(toast)* santé !
cheese le fromage
chemist's la pharmacie
cheque le chèque
cheque book le carnet de chèques
cheque card la carte bancaire
cherry la cerise
chess les échecs
chest la poitrine
chest of drawers la commode
chicken le poulet
child l'enfant
children les enfants
china la porcelaine
chips les frites
chocolate le chocolat
  a box of chocolates une boîte de chocolats
chop *(food)* la côtelette
  (verb: cut) couper
Christian name le prénom
church l'église
cigar le cigar
cigarette la cigarette
cinema le cinéma
city la ville
city centre le centre ville
class la classe
classical music la musique classique

clean propre
clear clair
clever intelligent
cling film le film alimentaire transparent
clock l'horloge
close *(near)* près
  (stuffy) étouffant
  (verb) fermer
closed fermé
clothes les vêtements
clubs *(cards)* trèfles
clutch l'embrayage
coach le car
  (train) le wagon
coach station la gare routière
coat le manteau
coathanger le cintre
cockroach le cafard
coffee le café
coin la pièce
cold *(illness)* le rhume
  (adj) froid
collar le col
collection *(stamps etc)* la collection
  (postal) la levée
colour la couleur
colour film la pellicule couleur
comb *(noun)* le peigne
  (verb) peigner
come venir
  I come from ... je viens de ...
  we came last week nous sommes arrivés la semaine dernière
Common Market le Marché commun
compact disc le disque compact
compartment le compartiment
complicated compliqué
computer l'ordinateur
concert le concert
conditioner *(hair)* le baume après-shampooing

125

condom le préservatif
conductor *(bus)* le receveur
  (orchestra) le chef d'orchestre
congratulations! félicitations !
consulate le consulat
contact lenses les verres de
  contact
contraceptive le contraceptif
cook *(noun)* le cuisinier
  (female) la cuisinière
  (verb) faire la cuisine
cooker la cuisinière
cooking utensils les ustensiles de
  cuisine
cool frais, *(fem)* fraîche
cork le bouchon
corkscrew le tire-bouchon
corner le coin
corridor le couloir
Corsica la Corse
Corsican corse
  (man) un Corse
  (woman) une Corse
cosmetics les produits de beauté
cost *(verb)* coûter
  what does it cost? combien ça
  coûte ?
cotton le coton
cotton wool le coton hydrophile
cough *(noun)* la toux
  (verb) tousser
country *(state)* le pays
  (not town) la campagne
cousin le cousin
  (female) la cousine
crab le crabe
cramp la crampe
crayfish *(freshwater)* l'écrevisse
  (saltwater) la langoustine
cream la crème
credit card la carte de crédit
crisps les chips
crowded bondé
cruise la croisière

crutches les béquilles
cry *(weep)* pleurer
  (shout) crier
cucumber le concombre
cufflinks les boutons de manchette
cup la tasse
cupboard le placard
curlers les rouleaux
curls les boucles
current le courant
curry le curry
curtain le rideau
Customs la douane
cut *(noun)* la coupure
  (verb) couper

dad papa
dance *(noun)* la danse
  (verb) danser
dangerous dangereux
dark foncé
  dark blue bleu foncé
daughter la fille
day le jour
dead mort
deaf sourd
dear cher
deckchair le transat
deep profond
delay *(noun)* le retard
deliberately exprès
dentist le/la dentiste
dentures le dentier
deny nier
deodorant le déodorant
department store le grand
  magasin
departure le départ
develop développer
diamond *(jewel)* le diamant
diamonds *(cards)* carreaux
diary l'agenda
dictionary le dictionnaire
die mourir

iesel le diesel
ifferent différent
that's different c'est différent
I'd like a different one j'en voudrais un autre
ifficult difficile
ining room la salle à manger
irectory *(telephone)* l'annuaire
isabled handicapé
isposable nappies les couches à jeter
istributor *(car)* le delco
ive *(verb)* plonger
iving board le plongeoir
ivorced divorcé
o faire
how do you do? comment allez-vous ?
octor le docteur
(female) la doctoresse
ocument le document
og le chien
oll la poupée
ollar le dollar
oor la porte
ouble room une chambre pour deux personnes
oughnut le beignet
own en bas
rawing pin la punaise
ress la robe
rink *(noun)* la boisson
(verb) boire
would you like a drink? voulez-vous boire quelque chose ?
rinking water l'eau potable
rive *(verb: car)* conduire
river le conducteur
(female) la conductrice
riving licence le permis de conduire
runk soûl, ivre
ry sec, *(fem)* sèche
ry cleaner's le pressing

during pendant
dustbin la poubelle
duster le chiffon à poussière
duty-free hors-taxe
duvet la couette

each *(every)* chaque
two francs each deux francs pièce
ear l'oreille
early tôt
earrings les boucles d'oreille
east l'est
easy facile
eat manger
EC la C.E.E.
egg l'œuf
either: either of them n'importe lequel
either ... or ... soit ... soit ...
elastic élastique
elastic band l'élastique
elbows les coudes
electric électrique
electricity l'électricité
else: something else autre chose
someone else quelqu'un d'autre
somewhere else ailleurs
embarrassing gênant
embassy l'ambassade
embroidery la broderie
emerald l'émeraude
emergency l'urgence
emergency cord le cordon d'alarme
emergency exit la sortie de secours
empty vide
end la fin
engaged *(couple)* fiancé
(occupied) occupé
engine *(motor)* le moteur
(railway) la locomotive
England l'Angleterre

English anglais
Englishman un Anglais
Englishwoman une Anglaise
enlargement l'agrandissement
enough assez
entertainment le divertissement
entrance l'entrée
envelope l'enveloppe
escalator l'escalier roulant
especially particulièrement
evening le soir
every chaque
everyone tout le monde
everything tout
everywhere partout
example l'exemple
  for example par exemple
excellent excellent
excess baggage l'excédent de
  bagages
exchange *(verb)* échanger
exchange rate le taux de change
excursion l'excursion
excuse me! pardon !
exit la sortie
expensive cher
extension lead la rallonge
eye l'œil
  eyes les yeux

face le visage
faint vague
  to faint evanouir
fair *(noun)* la foire
  (just) juste
  it's not fair ce n'est pas juste
fan *(ventilator)* le ventilateur
  (enthusiast) le/la fan
fan belt la courroie du ventilateur
fantastic fantastique
far loin
  how far is it to …? est-ce que …
  est loin d'ici ?
fare le prix du billet

farm la ferme
farmer le fermier
fashion la mode
fast rapide
fat *(of person)* gros, *(fem)* grosse
  (on meat etc) le gras
father le père
fax *(noun)* le fax
  (verb: document) faxer
feel *(touch)* toucher
  I feel hot j'ai chaud
  I feel like … j'ai envie de …
  I don't feel well je ne me sens
  pas bien
feet les pieds
felt-tip pen le feutre
ferry *(small)* le bac
  (large) le ferry
fever la fièvre
fiancé le fiancé
fiancée la fiancée
field le champ
fig la figue
filling *(in tooth)* le plombage
  (in sandwich, cake) la garniture
film le film
filter paper le papier filtre
finger le doigt
fire le feu
  (blaze) l'incendie
fire extinguisher l'extincteur
fireworks le feu d'artifice
first premier
first aid les premiers soins
first floor le premier étage
fish le poisson
fishing la pêche
  to go fishing aller à la pêche
fishing rod la canne à pêche
fishmonger's la poissonnerie
fizzy pétillant
flag le drapeau
flash *(camera)* le flash
flat *(level)* plat

(apartment) l'appartement

avour le goût

ea la puce

ight le vol

ip-flops les tongs

ippers les palmes

oor *(ground)* le plancher

(storey) l'étage

our la farine

ower la fleur

ute la flûte

y *(insect)* la mouche

(verb: of plane etc) voler

(of person) prendre l'avion

og le brouillard

olk music la musique folklorique

ood la nourriture

ood poisoning l'intoxication
  alimentaire

oot le pied

ootball le football

or pour

  for me pour moi

  what for? pour quoi faire ?

  for a week pour une semaine

oreigner l'étranger

  (female) l'étrangère

orest la forêt

orget oublier

ork la fourchette

ortnight quinze jours

ountain pen le stylo-plume

ourth quatrième

France la France

free *(no cost)* gratuit

  (at liberty) libre

freezer le congélateur

French français

  the French les Français

Frenchman un Français

Frenchwoman une Française

fridge le frigo

friend l'ami

  (female) l'amie

friendly amical

fringe la frange

front: in front devant

frost le gel

fruit le fruit

fruit juice le jus de fruit

fry frire

frying pan la poêle

full complet

  I'm full! j'ai l'estomac bien
  rempli !

full board la pension complète

funny drôle

furniture les meubles

garage le garage

garden le jardin

garlic l'ail

gas-permeable lenses les lentilles
  semi-souples

gate le portail, la grille

  (at airport) la porte

gay homosexuel

gear *(car)* la vitesse

gear lever le levier de vitesse

gel le gel

gents *(toilet)* les toilettes pour
  hommes

German allemand

  (man) un Allemand

  (woman) une Allemande

Germany l'Allemagne

get *(fetch)* aller chercher

  have you got ...? avez-vous ... ?

  to get the train prendre le train

get back: we get back tomorrow
  nous rentrons demain

  to get something back récupérer
  quelque chose

get in entrer

  (arrive) arriver

get off *(bus etc)* descendre

get on *(bus etc)* monter

get out sortir

get up se lever
gift le cadeau
gin le gin
ginger le gingembre
girl *(child)* la fille
  (young woman) la jeune fille
girlfriend la petite amie
give donner
glad heureux
glass le verre
glasses les lunettes
gloss prints les épreuves sur papier
  glacé
gloves les gants
glue la colle
go aller
gold l'or
good bon, *(fem)* bonne
  good! bien !
goodbye au revoir
government le gouvernement
granddaughter la petite-fille
grandfather le grand-père
grandmother la grand-mère
grandson le petit-fils
grandparents les grands-parents
grape(s) le raisin
grass l'herbe
Great Britain la Grande-Bretagne
green vert
grey gris
grill le gril
grocer's l'épicerie
ground floor le rez-de-chaussée
ground sheet le tapis de sol
guarantee *(noun)* la garantie
  (verb) garantir
guard *(train)* le chef de train
guide le/la guide
guide book le guide
guitar la guitare
gun *(rifle)* le fusil
  (pistol) le pistolet

hair les cheveux
haircut la coupe (de cheveux)
hairdresser le coiffeur
  (female) la coiffeuse
hair dryer le sèche-cheveux
hair spray la laque
half demi
  half an hour une demi-heure
half board la demi-pension
ham le jambon
hamburger le hamburger
hammer le marteau
hand la main
handbag le sac à main
handbrake le frein à main
handkerchief le mouchoir
handle *(door)* la poignée
handsome beau
hangover la gueule de bois
happy heureux
harbour le port
hard dur
  (difficult) difficile
hard lenses les lentilles rigides
hardware shop la quincaillerie
hat le chapeau
have avoir
  have you got ...? avez-vous ... ?
hayfever le rhume des foins
he il
head la tête
headache le mal de tête
headlights les phares
hear entendre
hearing aid l'appareil acoustique
heart le cœur
hearts *(cards)* cœurs
heater le radiateur
heating le chauffage
heavy lourd
heel le talon
hello bonjour
help *(noun)* l'aide
  (verb) aider

her: it's her c'est elle
  it's for her c'est pour elle
  give it to her donnez-le lui
  her book son livre
  her house sa maison
  her shoes ses chaussures
  it's hers c'est à elle
hi salut
high haut
highway code le code de la route
hill la colline
him: it's him c'est lui
  it's for him c'est pour lui
  give it to him donnez-le lui
hire: for hire à louer
his: his book son livre
  his house sa maison
  his shoes ses chaussures
  it's his c'est à lui
history l'histoire
hitchhike faire de l'autostop
hobby le passe-temps
holiday les vacances
home: at home *(my home)* chez
  moi
  he's at home il est chez lui
honest honnête
honey le miel
honeymoon la lune de miel
horn *(car)* le klaxon
  (animal) la corne
horrible horrible
hospital l'hôpital
hot chaud
hour l'heure
house la maison
hovercraft l'aéroglisseur
hoverport l'hoverport
how? comment ?
hungry: I'm hungry j'ai faim
hurry: I'm in a hurry je suis
  pressé
husband le mari
hydrofoil l'hydrofoil

I je
ice la glace
ice cream la glace
ice lolly l'esquimau
ice rink la patinoire
ice-skates les patins à glace
ice-skating: to go ice-skating
  aller patiner
if si
ignition l'allumage
ill malade
immediately immédiatement
impossible impossible
in dans
  in France en France
indicator le clignotant
indigestion l'indigestion
infection l'infection
information l'information
injection la piqûre
injury la blessure
ink l'encre
inn l'auberge
inner tube la chambre à air
insect l'insecte
insect repellent la crème anti-
  insecte
insomnia l'insomnie
instant coffee le café soluble
insurance l'assurance
interesting intéressant
interpret interpréter
interpreter l'interprète
invitation l'invitation
Ireland l'Irlande
Irish irlandais
  (man) un Irlandais
  (woman) une Irlandaise
iron *(metal)* le fer
  (for clothes) le fer à repasser
  (verb) repasser
is: he/she is il/elle est
  it is c'est
island l'île

131

it il; elle
Italian italien
  (man) un Italien
  (woman) une Italienne
Italy l'Italie
its son; sa; ses *(see his)*

jacket la veste
jam la confiture
jazz le jazz
jeans les jeans
jellyfish la méduse
jetfoil le jetfoil
jeweller's la bijouterie
job le travail
jog *(verb)* faire du jogging
  to go for a jog aller faire du jogging
joke la plaisanterie
journey le voyage
jumper le pull
just: it's just arrived ça vient juste d'arriver
  I've just one left il ne m'en reste qu'un

kettle la bouilloire
key la clé
kidney le rein
kilo le kilo
kilometre le kilomètre
kitchen la cuisine
knee le genou
knife le couteau
knit tricoter
knitting needle l'aiguille à tricoter
know *(fact)* savoir
  (person) connaître
  I don't know je ne sais pas

label l'étiquette
lace la dentelle
  (of shoe) le lacet
ladies *(toilet)* les toilettes pour dames

lake le lac
lamb l'agneau
lamp la lampe
lampshade l'abat-jour
land *(noun)* la terre
  (verb) atterrir
language la langue
large grand
last *(final)* dernier
  last week la semaine dernière
  at last! enfin !
late tard
  the bus is late le bus est en retard
later plus tard
laugh rire
launderette la laverie automatique
laundry *(place)* la blanchisserie
  (clothes) le linge
laxative le laxatif
lazy paresseux
leaf la feuille
leaflet le dépliant
learn apprendre
leather le cuir
left *(not right)* la gauche
  there's nothing left il ne reste plus rien
left-luggage locker la consigne automatique
left-luggage office la consigne
leg la jambe
lemon le citron
lemonade la limonade
length la longueur
lens *(camera)* l'objectif
less moins
lesson la leçon
letter la lettre
letter box la boîte à lettres
lettuce la laitue
library la bibliothèque
licence le permis

life la vie
lift *(in building)* l'ascenseur
  could you give me a lift
  pourriez-vous m'emmener ?
light la lumière
  (not heavy) léger
  (not dark) clair
light bulb l'ampoule
light meter la cellule
  photoélectrique
lighter le briquet
lighter fuel le gaz à briquet
like: I like you je vous aime bien
  I like swimming j'aime nager
  it's like ... c'est comme ...
lime *(fruit)* le citron vert
lip salve le baume pour les lèvres
lipstick le rouge à lèvres
liqueur la liqueur
list la liste
litre le litre
litter les ordures
little *(small)* petit
  it's a little big c'est un peu trop
  grand
  just a little juste un peu
liver le foie
lobster le homard
lollipop la sucette
long long, *(fem)* longue
lorry le camion
lost property les objets trouvés
loud fort
  (colour) criard
lounge le salon
love *(noun)* l'amour
  (verb) aimer
lover l'amant
  (female) l'amante
low bas
luck la chance
  good luck! bonne chance !
luggage les bagages
luggage rack le porte-bagages

lunch le déjeuner
Luxembourg le Luxembourg

mad fou, *(fem)* folle
magazine la revue
maid la femme de chambre
mail le courrier
make faire
make-up le maquillage
man l'homme
manager le directeur
many: not many pas beaucoup
map la carte
  (street map) le plan
margarine la margarine
market le marché
marmalade la marmelade
  d'oranges
married marié
mascara le mascara
mass *(church)* la messe
mast le mât
match *(light)* l'allumette
  (sport) le match
material *(cloth)* le tissu
matter: it doesn't matter ça ne
  fait rien
mattress le matelas
maybe peut-être
me: it's me c'est moi
  it's for me c'est pour moi
  give it to me donnez-le-moi
meal le repas
mean: what does this mean?
  qu'est-ce que cela veut dire ?
meat la viande
mechanic le mécanicien
medicine le médicament
Mediterranean la Méditerranée
meeting la réunion
melon le melon
menu le menu
message le message
midday midi

middle le milieu
midnight minuit
milk le lait
mine: it's mine c'est à moi
mineral water l'eau minérale
minute *(noun)* la minute
mirror le miroir
  (car) le rétroviseur
Miss Mademoiselle
mistake l'erreur
money l'argent
month le mois
monument le monument
moon la lune
moped la mobylette ®
more plus
  more or less plus ou moins
morning le matin
  in the morning dans la matinée
Moroccan marocain
Morocco le Maroc
mosquito le moustique
mother la mère
motorbike la moto
motorboat le bateau à moteur
motorway l'autoroute
mountain la montagne
mountain bike le vélo tout terrain
mouse la souris
mousse *(hair)* la mousse
moustache la moustache
mouth la bouche
move bouger
  (house) déménager
  don't move! ne bougez pas !
Mr Monsieur
Mrs Madame
mug la tasse
mum maman
museum le musée
mushroom le champignon
music la musique
musical instrument l'instrument de musique

musician le musicien
mussels les moules
must: I must ... je dois ...
mustard la moutarde
my: my book mon livre
  my house ma maison
  my shoes mes chaussures

nail *(metal)* le clou
  (finger) l'ongle
nail clippers la pince à ongles
nail file la lime à ongles
nail polish le vernis à ongles
name le nom
  what's your name comment vous appelez-vous ?
nappy la couche
narrow étroit
near: near the door près de la porte
  near London près de Londres
necessary nécessaire
neck le cou
necklace le collier
need *(verb)* avoir besoin de
  I need ... j'ai besoin de ...
  there's no need ce n'est pas nécessaire
needle l'aiguille
negative *(photo)* le négatif
neither: neither of them ni l'un ni l'autre
  neither ... nor ... ni ... ni ...
nephew le neveu
never jamais
new nouveau, *(fem)* nouvelle
news les nouvelles
  (TV) les informations
newsagent le tabac-journaux
newspaper le journal
New Zealand la Nouvelle-Zélande
next prochain
  next week la semaine prochaine
  what next? et puis quoi ?

nice *(place etc)* joli
  (person) sympathique
  (to eat) bon
niece la nièce
night la nuit
nightclub la boîte de nuit
nightdress la chemise de nuit
no *(response)* non
  (not any) aucun
  he's not ... il n'est pas ...
nobody personne
noisy bruyant
none aucun
north le nord
Northern Ireland l'Irlande du
  Nord
nose le nez
not pas
  he's not ... il n'est pas ...
notebook le carnet
nothing rien
novel le roman
now maintenant
nowhere nulle part
nudist le nudiste
number *(figure)* le numéro
  (amount) le nombre
number plate la plaque
  d'immatriculation
nursery slope la piste pour
  débutants
nut *(fruit)* la noix
  (for bolt) l'écrou

oars les rames
occasionally de temps en temps
of de
office le bureau
often souvent
oil l'huile
ointment la pommade
OK d'accord
old vieux, *(fem)* vieille
  how old are you? quel âge avez-
  vous ?

olive l'olive
omelette l'omelette
on ... sur ...
one un/une
onion l'oignon
only seulement
open *(adj)* ouvert
  (verb) ouvrir
operation l'opération
operator *(phone)* l'opérateur
  (female) l'opératrice
opposite en face
optician's l'opticien
or ou
orange *(fruit)* l'orange
  (colour) orange
orange juice le jus d'orange
orchestra l'orchestre
ordinary habituel
organ *(music)* l'orgue
other: the other ... l'autre ...
our: our house notre maison
  our children nos enfants
  it's ours c'est à nous
out: he's out il n'est pas là
outside dehors
oven le four
over *(above)* au-dessus de
  (more than) plus de
  (finished) fini
  it's over the road c'est de l'autre
  côté de la rue
  over there là-bas
overtake doubler
oyster l'huître

pack of cards le jeu de cartes
package le paquet
  (parcel) le colis
packet le paquet
padlock un cadenas
page la page
pain la douleur
paint *(noun)* la peinture

pair la paire
palace le palais
pale pâle, blême
pancake la crêpe
paper le papier
   (newspaper) le journal
paracetamol le comprimé de
   paracétamol
paraffin le pétrole
parcel le colis
pardon? pardon ?
parents les parents
park *(noun)* le jardin public
   (verb) garer
parsley le persil
parting *(hair)* la raie
party *(celebration)* une fête
   (group) le groupe
   (political) le parti
passenger le passager
passport le passeport
passport control le contrôle des
   passeports
pasta les pâtes
path le chemin
pavement le trottoir
pay payer
peach la pêche
peanuts les cacahuètes
pear la poire
pearl la perle
peas les petits pois
pedestrian le piéton
peg *(clothes)* la pince à linge
   (tent) le piquet de tente
pen le stylo
pencil le crayon
pencil sharpener le taille-crayon
penfriend le correspondant
   (female) la correspondante
penknife le canif
people les gens
pepper *(& salt)* le poivre
   (red/green) le poivron

peppermints les bonbons à la
   menthe
per: per night par nuit
perfect parfait
perfume le parfum
perhaps peut-être
perm la permanente
petrol l'essence
petrol station la station-service
photograph *(noun)* la photo
   (verb) photographier
photographer le/la photographe
phrase book un guide de
   conversation
piano le piano
pickpocket le pickpocket
picnic le pique-nique
piece le morceau
pillow l'oreiller
pilot le pilote
pin l'épingle
pineapple l'ananas
pink rose
pipe *(for smoking)* la pipe
   (for water) le tuyau
piston le piston
pizza la pizza
place l'endroit
   at your place chez vous
plant la plante
plaster *(for cut)* le pansement
plastic le plastique
plastic bag le sac en plastique
plate l'assiette
platform le quai
play *(noun: theatre)* la pièce
   (verb) jouer
please s'il vous plaît
plug *(electrical)* la prise
   (sink) le bouchon
pocket la poche
poison le poison
police la police
policeman le policier

police station le commissariat
politics la politique
poor pauvre
　(bad quality) mauvais
pop music la musique pop
pork le porc
port *(harbour)* le port
　(drink) le porto
porter le porteur
possible possible
post *(noun)* la poste
　(verb) poster
post box la boîte postale
postcard la carte postale
poster *(outside)* l'affiche
　(inside) le poster
postman le facteur
post office la poste
potato la pomme de terre
poultry la volaille
pound *(money, weight)* la livre
powder la poudre
pram le landau
prawn la crevette
prefer préférer
prescription l'ordonnance
pretty *(beautiful)* joli
　(quite) plutôt
priest le prêtre
private privé
problem le problème
public le public
pull tirer
puncture la crevaison
purple violet
purse le porte-monnaie
push pousser
pushchair la poussette
put mettre
pyjamas le pyjama
Pyrenees les Pyrénées

quality la qualité
quarter le quart

quay le quai
question la question
queue *(noun)* la queue
　(verb) faire la queue
quick rapide
quiet silencieux
quite *(fairly)* assez
　(fully) très

radiator le radiateur
radio la radio
radish le radis
rail: by rail par chemin de fer
railway le chemin de fer
rain la pluie
raincoat l'imperméable
raisin le raisin sec
rare *(uncommon)* rare
　(steak) bleu
raspberry la framboise
rat le rat
razor blades les lames de rasoir
read lire
reading lamp la lampe de bureau
　(bedside) la lampe de chevet
ready prêt
rear lights les feux arrière
receipt le reçu
receptionist le/la receptionniste
record *(music)* le disque
　(sporting etc) le record
record player le tourne-disque
record shop le disquaire
red rouge
　(hair) roux
refreshments les rafraîchissements
registered letter la lettre
　recommandée
relax se détendre
religion la religion
remember: I remember je m'en
　souviens
　I don't remember je ne me
　souviens pas

rent *(verb)* louer
reservation la réservation
rest *(remainder)* le reste
**(verb: relax)* se reposer
restaurant le restaurant
restaurant car le wagon-
restaurant
return *(come back)* revenir
(give back) rendre
return ticket l'aller retour
rice le riz
rich riche
right *(correct)* juste
(not left) la droite
ring *(wedding etc)* la bague
(verb: call) téléphoner
ripe mûr
river la rivière
(big) le fleuve
road la route
(in town) la rue
rock *(stone)* le rocher
(music) le rock
roll *(bread)* le petit pain
roof le toit
room la chambre
(space) la place
rope la corde
rose la rose
round *(circular)* rond
it's my round c'est ma tournée
row *(verb)* ramer
rowing boat la barque
rubber *(eraser)* la gomme
(material) le caoutchouc
rubbish les ordures
rucksack le sac à dos
rug *(mat)* la carpette
(blanket) la couverture
ruins les ruines
ruler la règle
rum le rhum
run *(verb)* courir
runway la piste

sad triste
safe *(not in danger)* en sécurité
(not dangerous) sans danger
safety pin l'épingle de nourrice
sailing boat le voilier
salad la salade
sale la vente
(at reduced prices) les soldes
salmon le saumon
salt le sel
same: the same ... le/la même ...
the same again, please la même
chose, s'il vous plaît
sand le sable
sandals les sandales
sand dunes les dunes
sandwich le sandwich
sanitary towels les serviettes
hygiéniques
sauce la sauce
saucepan la casserole
sauna le sauna
sausage la saucisse
say dire
what did you say? qu'avez-vous
dit ?
how do you say ...? comment
dit-on ... ?
scampi les langoustines
scarf l'écharpe
(head) le foulard
school l'école
scissors les ciseaux
Scotland l'Ecosse
Scotsman un Ecossais
Scotswoman une Ecossaise
Scottish écossais
screw la vis
screwdriver le tournevis
sea la mer
seafood les fruits de mer
seat la place
seat belt la ceinture de sécurité
second *(of time)* la seconde

(in series) deuxième
see voir
  I can't see je ne vois rien
  I see je vois
sell vendre
sellotape ® le scotch ®
separate *(adj)* séparé
  (verb) séparer
serious sérieux
several plusieurs
sew coudre
shampoo le shampooing
shave: to have a shave se raser
shaving foam la mousse à raser
shawl le châle
she elle
sheet le drap
shell la coquille
shellfish les crustacés
ship le bateau
shirt la chemise
shoe laces les lacets
shoe polish le cirage
shoes les chaussures
shop le magasin
shopping les courses
  to go shopping faire les courses
short court
shorts le short
shoulder l'épaule
shower *(bath)* la douche
  (rain) l'averse
shrimp la crevette
shutter *(camera)* l'obturateur
  (window) le volet
sick: I feel sick j'ai envie de vomir
  to be sick *(vomit)* vomir
side *(edge)* le bord
sidelights les feux de position
sights: the sights of Paris les
  vues de Paris
silk la soie
silver *(colour)* argenté
  (metal) l'argent

simple simple
sing chanter
single *(one)* seul
  (unmarried) célibataire
single room la chambre pour une
  personne
sister la sœur
skates les patins à glace
ski *(noun)* le ski
  (verb) skier
ski boots les chaussures de ski
skid *(verb)* déraper
skiing: to go skiing faire du ski
ski lift le remonte-pente
skin cleanser le démaquillant
ski resort la station de ski
skirt la jupe
ski stick le bâton de ski
sky le ciel
sledge la luge
sleep *(noun)* le sommeil
  (verb) dormir
sleeper le wagon-lit
sleeping bag le sac de couchage
sleeping pill le somnifère
slippers les pantoufles
slow lent
small petit
smell *(noun)* l'odeur
  (verb) sentir
smile *(noun)* le sourire
  (verb) sourire
smoke *(noun)* la fumée
  (verb) fumer
snack le snack
snow la neige
so si
soaking solution *(for contact lenses)*
  la solution de trempage
soap le savon
socks les chaussettes
soda water l'eau gazeuse
soft lenses les lentilles souples
somebody quelqu'un

somehow d'une façon ou d'une autre
something quelque chose
sometimes quelquefois
somewhere quelque part
son le fils
song la chanson
sorry! *(apology)* pardon !
  sorry? *(pardon?)* pardon ?
  I'm sorry je suis désolé
soup la soupe
south le sud
South Africa l'Afrique du Sud
souvenir le souvenir
spade *(shovel)* la pelle
spades *(cards)* piques
Spain l'Espagne
Spanish espagnol
spanner la clé anglaise
spares les pièces de rechange
spark(ing) plug la bougie
speak parler
  do you speak ...? parlez-vous ... ?
  I don't speak ... je ne parle pas ...
speed la vitesse
speed limit la limitation de vitesse
spider l'araignée
spinach les épinards
spoon la cuillère
sports centre le centre sportif
spring *(mechanical)* le ressort
  (season) le printemps
square *(noun: in town)* la place
  (adj: shape) carré
stadium le stade
staircase l'escalier
stairs les escaliers
stamp le timbre
stapler l'agrafeuse
star l'étoile
  (film) la vedette
start *(noun: beginning)* le début
  (verb) commencer

station la gare
  (underground) la station
statue la statue
steak le steak
steal voler
  it's been stolen on l'a volé
steamer le bateau à vapeur
  (cooking) le couscoussier
steering wheel le volant
sting *(noun)* la piqûre
  (verb) piquer
stockings les bas
stomach l'estomac
stomach ache le mal de ventre
stop *(noun: bus)* l'arrêt (de bus)
  (verb) s'arrêter
  stop! stop !
storm la tempête
strawberry la fraise
stream *(small river)* le ruisseau
street la rue
string *(cord)* la ficelle
  (guitar etc) la corde
strong *(person, drink)* fort
  (material) résistant
student l'étudiant
  (female) l'étudiante
stupid stupide
suburbs la banlieue
sugar le sucre
suit *(noun)* le costume
  it suits you ça vous va bien
suitcase la valise
sun le soleil
sunbathe se faire bronzer
sunburn le coup de soleil
sunglasses les lunettes de soleil
sunny ensoleillé
sunshade le parasol
suntan le bronzage
suntan lotion la lotion solaire
supermarket le supermarché
supper le souper
supplement le supplément

sure sûr
surname le nom de famille
sweat *(noun)* la transpiration
  (verb) transpirer
sweatshirt le sweat-shirt
sweet *(not sour)* sucré
  (candy) le bonbon
swim *(verb)* nager
swimming: to go swimming aller
  se baigner
swimming costume le maillot de
  bain
swimming pool la piscine
swimming trunks le maillot de
  bain
Swiss suisse
  (man) le Suisse
  (woman) la Suissesse
switch l'interrupteur
Switzerland la Suisse
synagogue la synagogue

table la table
tablet le comprimé
take prendre
take away: to take away à
  emporter
take-off *(noun)* le décollage
talcum powder le talc
talk *(noun)* la conversation
  (verb) parler
tall grand
tampon le tampon
tangerine la mandarine
tap le robinet
tapestry la tapisserie
tea le thé
teacher *(secondary)* le professeur
tea towel le torchon
telegram le télégramme
telephone *(noun)* le téléphone
  (verb) téléphoner
telephone box la cabine
  téléphonique

television la télévision
temperature la température
tent la tente
tent pole le montant de tente
than que
thank *(verb)* remercier
  thank you merci
  thanks merci
that *(that one)* ça
  that bus ce bus
  that man cet homme
  that woman cette femme
  what's that? qu'est-ce que c'est ?
  I think that the ... je pense que
  le ...
the le/la; *(plural)* les *(see p 5)*
their: their room leur chambre
  their books leurs livres
  it's theirs c'est à eux
them: it's them ce sont eux/elles
  it's for them c'est pour eux/elles
  give it to them donnez-le-leur
then alors
  (after) ensuite
there là
  there is/are ... il y a ...
  is/are there ...? y a-t-il ... ?
Thermos flask ® la bouteille
  thermos
these: these things ces choses
  these are mine ils sont à moi
they ils; *(fem)* elles
thick épais
thin mince
think penser
  I think so je pense que oui
  I'll think about it je vais y
  penser
third troisième
thirsty: I'm thirsty j'ai soif
this *(this one)* ceci
  this bus ce bus
  this man cet homme
  this woman cette femme

what's this? qu'est-ce que c'est ?
this is Mr ... je vous présente
M. ...
those: those things ces choses-là
those are his ils sont à lui
throat la gorge
throat pastilles les pastilles pour la
gorge
through à travers
thunderstorm l'orage
ticket le billet
(underground, bus) le ticket
ticket collector le contrôleur
ticket office la billetterie
tide la marée
tie *(noun)* la cravate
(verb) nouer
tight étroit
tights les collants
time l'heure
what's the time? quelle heure
est-il ?
timetable *(train, bus)* l'horaire
tin la boîte de conserve
tin-opener l'ouvre-boîte
tip *(money)* le pourboire
(end) le bout
tired fatigué
tissues les kleenex ®
to: to England en Angleterre
to Paris à Paris
to the station à la gare
to the centre au centre
to the doctor chez le docteur
toast le pain grillé
tobacco le tabac
toboggan le toboggan
today aujourd'hui
together ensemble
toilet les toilettes
toilet paper le papier hygiénique
tomato la tomate
tomorrow demain
tongue la langue

tonic le tonic
tonight ce soir
too *(also)* aussi
(excessively) trop
tooth la dent
toothache le mal de dents
toothbrush la brosse à dents
toothpaste le dentifrice
torch la lampe de poche
tour la visite
tourist le/la touriste
tourist office le syndicat
d'initiative
towel la serviette
tower la tour
town la ville
town hall l'hôtel de ville
toy le jouet
track suit le survêtement
tractor le tracteur
tradition la tradition
traffic la circulation, le trafic
traffic lights les feux
trailer la remorque
train le train
trainers les tennis
translate traduire
translator le traducteur
(female) la traductrice
travel agency l'agence de voyages
traveller's cheque le chèque de
voyage
tray le plateau
tree l'arbre
trousers le pantalon
truck le camion
true vrai
try essayer
Tunisia la Tunisie
Tunisian tunisien
tunnel le tunnel
tweezers la pince à épiler
typewriter la machine à écrire
tyre le pneu

umbrella le parapluie
uncle l'oncle
under ... sous ...
underground le métro
underpants le slip
underskirt le jupon
understand comprendre
  I understand je comprends
  I don't understand je ne
  comprends pas
underwear les sous-vêtements
university l'université
unleaded sans plomb
until jusqu'à
unusual inhabituel
up en haut
  (upwards) vers le haut
  up there là-haut
urgent urgent
us: it's us c'est nous
  it's for us c'est pour nous
  give it to us donnez-le-nous
use *(verb)* utiliser
  it's no use ça ne sert à rien
useful utile
usual habituel
usually d'habitude

vacancy *(room)* la chambre à
louer
vacuum cleaner l'aspirateur
valley la vallée
valve la soupape
vanilla la vanille
vase le vase
veal le veau
vegetables les légumes
vegetarian *(adj)* végétarien
vehicle le véhicule
very très
  very much beaucoup
vest le tricot de corps
video *(film/tape)* la vidéo
video recorder le magnétoscope

view la vue
viewfinder le viseur
villa la villa
village le village
vinegar le vinaigre
violin le violon
visit *(noun)* la visite
  (verb: place) visiter
  (person) rendre visite
visitor le visiteur
  (female) la visiteuse
vitamin tablet le comprimé de
vitamines
vodka la vodka
voice la voix

wait attendre
  wait! attendez !
waiter le serveur
  waiter! garçon !
waiting room la salle d'attente
waitress la serveuse
  waitress! Mademoiselle !
Wales le pays de Galles
walk *(verb)* marcher
  to go for a walk aller se
  promener
walkman ® le walkman ®, le
baladeur
wall *(inside)* la paroi
  (outside) le mur
wallet le portefeuille
war la guerre
wardrobe l'armoire
warm chaud
was: I was j'étais
  he was il était
  she was elle était
  it was il/elle était
washer la rondelle
washing powder la lessive
washing-up liquid le produit pour
la vaisselle
wasp la guêpe

143

watch *(noun)* la montre
  (verb) regarder
water l'eau
water heater le chauffe-eau
waterfall la chute d'eau
wave *(noun)* la vague
  (verb) faire signe de la main
wavy *(hair)* ondulé
we nous
weather le temps
wedding le mariage
week la semaine
welcome: you're welcome je vous
  en prie
wellingtons les bottes en
  caoutchouc
Welsh gallois
Welshman un Gallois
Welshwoman une Galloise
were: we were nous étions
  you were vous étiez
  they were ils/elles étaient
west l'ouest
wet mouillé
what? comment ?
  what is it? qu'est-ce que c'est ?
wheel la roue
wheelchair le fauteuil roulant
when? quand ?
where? où ?
whether si
which? lequel ?
whisky le whisky
white blanc, *(fem)* blanche
who? qui ?
why? pourquoi ?
wide large
wife la femme
wind le vent
window la fenêtre
wine le vin
wine list la carte des vins

wine merchant le négociant en
  vins
wing l'aile
with avec
without sans
woman la femme
wood le bois
wool la laine
word le mot
work *(noun)* le travail
  (verb) travailler
  (machine etc) fonctionner
worse pire
worst le pire
wrapping paper le papier
  d'emballage
  (for presents) le papier cadeau
wrist le poignet
writing paper le papier à lettres
wrong faux, *(fem)* fausse

year l'année
yellow jaune
yes oui
yesterday hier
yet déjà
  not yet pas encore
yoghurt le yaourt
you vous
  (singular, familiar) tu
your: your house votre maison
  your shoes vos chaussures
  it's yours c'est à vous
  (singular, familiar)
  your book ton livre
  your house ta maison
  your shoes tes chaussures
  it's yours c'est à toi
youth hostel l'auberge de jeunesse

zip la fermeture éclair ®
zoo le zoo